THE PIONEERS
OF LAKE VIEW

THE PIONEERS OF LAKE VIEW

**A GUIDE TO SEATTLE'S
EARLY SETTLERS AND
THEIR CEMETERY**

BY ROBERT L. FERGUSON

Thistle Press

Ferguson, Robert Lewis

Edited by Duse McLean
Illustrations by E.B. Pete McLean
Design by Magrit Baurecht
Cover illustration by Margaret Chodos-Irvine
Back cover photo by Rick Carroll

The pioneers of lake view: a guide to Seattle's early
    settlers and their cemetery
Includes index

ISBN 0-9621935-4-2
Library of Congress number: 95-060729

Library of Congress Cataloguing-in-Publication Data
1. Pioneers—Washington (State)—Seattle—
    Biography. 2. Lake View Cemetery (Seattle,
    Washington)—Guidebooks

Published by Thistle Press
P.O. Box 732
Bellevue, WA 98009
(206) 885-3173

ACKNOWLEDGEMENTS

A book about a cemetery might sound like it would be about dead people and death, but that's not the case. This book is about life and how our Northwest pioneers lived it.

Creating *The Pioneers of Lake View* has been a lively process, involving the talents, wisdom and cooperation of many people who got caught up in what appeared to be an offbeat project and helped make it finished book.

Thanks to the staff of the Museum of History and Industry (MOHAI), especially Rick Caldwell in the library for furnishing much needed records to track down obscure references. In addition, MOHAI has been enthusiastic about the project and has sponsored Walking Tours of Lake View to its membership.

The staff of the University of Washington Special Collections Library in Suzzallo spent many hours helping with background research on the pioneers.

Although this is a slim book, many technological wizards have played crucial roles in its production, starting with Cheryl Nodland at Computemps, who brought the pages into the computer. Lynn Meade of Desktop Connexion drew the hundreds of little squares to create the new, legible map of Lake View, while her husband, Mike, scanned in the drawings to their best advantage.

Many people involved with the book visited Lake View for the first time because of it. Pete McLean first became acquainted with the book on one of Robert's cemetery tours and returned many times to check on details for his illustrations. Rick Carroll braved blustery spring storms to take photos for the back cover, running for cover between shots. Margaret Chodos-Irvine spent days walking around the cemetery to get the right feel for her dramatic cover illustration. Magrit Baurecht, whose graphic design brought the many pieces of the book together, learned about the original denizens of Pioneer Square. And finally, Eileen Cavanagh combed through the text and cleaned up the loose ends with her expert editing.

So, to all the people whose lives are in this book, and to all the people who made it possible to do this book, our thanks.

PREFACE

I suppose this is the place to confess that I have for years been one of those slightly peculiar people who like to explore old cemeteries. I never spoke of my interest, even with family or friends. I guess it all seemed slightly creepy, even to me. I have observed fellow aficionados, exploring away like mad in cemeteries all over the world, but I have noticed that we almost never speak to one another, such is our secret shame at our compelling interest.

I am a native-born son of Seattle who, until about 1970, never had much interest in the pioneer history of Seattle. All that changed when I discovered Lake View Cemetery. For me it was the beginning of a twenty-five-year quest to discover the names, the stories, and finally the graves of the pioneer founders of the city. In the course of my searching, I have studied the entire available bibliography on pioneer history, including archives, museum collections, documents, deeds, and personal interviews with the living descendants of pioneer families. The study of pioneer history has enriched my life and I happily pass on to you what I have learned from my studies.

This book is dedicated to my mother and father, Enid and Sidney Harold Ferguson Sr., with my love and grateful appreciation.

TABLE OF CONTENTS

ILLUSTRATIONS

CHRONOLOGY
OF PIONEER SEATTLE

1845

International treaty establishes border between Canada and the U.S. at present latitude

SUMMER 1850

John Holgate and William Latimer spend the summer on Elliott Bay

SEPTEMBER 14 1851

The first homestead claims are made within the present-day city of Seattle

NOVEMBER 13 1851

The Denny Party, made up of Denny, Boren and Bell families, arrives at Alki Beach on West Seattle

FEBRUARY 1852

Dennys, Borens and Bells make homestead claims on the eastern shore of Elliott Bay, site of present-day downtown Seattle

MARCH 31 1852

Doc Maynard arrives, names the settlement "Seattle" after the local Indian chief

OCTOBER 1852

Henry Yesler arrives, establishes the first steampowered sawmill on Puget Sound

SUMMER 1853

Members of the Bethel Wagon Train begin arriving in Seattle

JANUARY 21 1855

Signing of The Treaty of Point Elliott. U.S. government takes legal title to land around Elliott Bay

WINTER-SPRING 1855-1856	Armed hostilities erupt between the Native Americans and white settlers on Puget Sound
JANUARY 26 1856	The Battle of Seattle, a one-day skirmish on Elliott Bay between the Native Americans and white settlers
OCTOBER 1860	The Rev. Daniel Bagley begins efforts to build the Territorial University
NOVEMBER 1860	Abraham Lincoln elected U.S. president, followed by the outbreak of the Civil War
APRIL 1865	Civil War ends, Lincoln assassinated. Reconstruction of the Union begins
JULY 14 1873	Tacoma selected as the terminus of the northern transcontinental railroad
JUNE 1887	The Northern Pacific Railroad arrives in Seattle
JUNE 6 1889	The Great Seattle Fire destroys the central business district. Modern city of Seattle rises from the ashes
APRIL 1893	New York Stock Market collapses, causing national financial depression
JULY 1897	Discovery of gold begins the Alaska-Yukon Gold Rush

The Pioneers

Today, nearly one hundred fifty years after the founding of the city of Seattle, a lively, if pedantic, debate continues as to when and where, what and by whom constitutes the founding of the city.

Seattle school children are taught from an early age that the founding occurred on the morning of November 13, 1851, when the schooner *Exact*, bound from Portland, Oregon Territory, disembarked a party of twenty-four men, women and children onto the shores of Alki beach. Four young families, the Dennys, Borens, Bells and Lows, and two brothers, Charles and Lee Terry, are generally assigned the credit for the founding of Seattle, but they were not the first white Americans to settle on the land surrounding Elliott Bay.

In the summer of 1850, two men, John Holgate and William Guthrie Latimer, lived on the shores of Elliott Bay. Both later returned with their families to take up permanent residence in the city. In September 1851, Jacob Maple and Henry Van Asselt made homestead claims on the banks of the Duwamish River near the site of the present neighborhood of Georgetown, the first claims within the present-day city of Seattle. In the following spring of 1852, the Denny, Boren and Bell families decamped from Alki to take up land claims on the eastern shores of Elliott Bay. Dr. David S. Maynard arrived soon after, on March 31, 1852. It was Doc Maynard who later named Seattle, which had been called Duwamps, in honor of his friend, the Indian Chief Sealth.

Seattle's first industry arrived in the spring of 1853, when Henry Yesler secured a site on the Seattle waterfront for his sawmill, the first steam-powered mill on Puget Sound. It was not until

January 21, 1855, with the signing of The Treaty of Point Elliott, that legal title to the land surrounding Elliott Bay was transferred from the original Native American inhabitants to the United States Government. The further development of Seattle was stalled for the next ten years, first by the outbreak of armed hostilities between the Native Americans and the pioneers in the winter of 1855-1856, then by the outbreak of the American Civil War in 1861. A brief spurt of growth occurred in 1860, with the construction of the grandiose Territorial University. The enormous structure stood on the present site of the Olympic Four Seasons Hotel. Virtually unused for the next ten years, it dominated the Seattle skyline for nearly fifty years.

In 1870 Seattle was still a small town with a population of only eleven hundred people. But slowly and methodically, it became the center of manufacturing, distribution and transportation on Puget Sound. Even the selection of Tacoma as the terminus of the transcontinental railroad failed to impede the growth of Seattle. When the railroads arrived in the late 1880s, the pioneer era came to an end. By the time of the Great Seattle Fire of June 6, 1889, Seattle had a population of forty thousand people and was poised for an explosion of growth in the following decades. The pioneer vision of Seattle as the dominant city of the Pacific Northwest had, in fact, come to pass, well within the lifetimes of many of its pioneer founders.

LAKE VIEW CEMETERY

Lake View Cemetery is a very average sort of American cemetery and its appeal is almost entirely local. With a few notable exceptions, Lake View is the final resting place for virtually all the pioneers of Seattle.

While a grave at Lake View may possess a certain panache in Seattle, it pales in comparison to the world's great cemeteries: The necropolis of Pere Lachaise in Paris, the hauntingly romantic High Gate Cemetery of London, or even the extravagant exhibitionism of Hollywood Memorial Park in Los Angeles. All of these cemeteries (Lake View included), however, have more in common than may be evident to the casual observer, for all are essentially Victorian cemeteries.

Prior to the nineteenth century, burial of the dead took place at home in rural areas or in parish churchyards in villages and cities. Expanding populations, high mortality rates and a casual attitude toward the disposition of human remains resulted in ghastly abuse of the dead and serious health and sanitation problems. In London it was not uncommon to have as many as eighteen burials in a single grave site. As churchyards rapidly filled, older graves were removed and the ground used again.

By 1830, the situation had become intolerable and public outcry led to a revolution in burial practices. In place of the charnel house atmosphere of the urban churchyard and popular abhorrence of the corpse, there emerged the Victorian concept of "The Beautiful Death." The dead were now thought of as sleeping in peace, awaiting a final judgment in beautiful repose. A person's grave became a permanent shrine, marked in eternal materials. Nineteenth century materialism propelled memorial architecture into ever grander statements of marble, granite and bronze.

As early as 1855, graves were dug on the east side of Maynard's Point, near the present-day intersection of Occidental Avenue South and Yesler Way. Later, burials took place at The White Church, Seattle's first church, at the corner of Second Avenue and Columbia Street. In 1863, David T. Denny and his wife, Louisa Boren Denny, donated land for use as a cemetery on the north edge of the Denny Regrade. Known as The Old Seattle Cemetery, it was in use until 1884, when it was converted into Denny Park.

Lake View Cemetery was established in 1872 when members of the St. John's Lodge of the Order of Freemasonry acquired the land from Doc Maynard for use as a Masonic Cemetery.

The land that is now Lake View Cemetery was located a long way from the small town of Seattle on the shores of Elliott Bay. When Doc Maynard died on March 13, 1873, his actual burial was delayed more than a month while a road was built to reach the new cemetery. From the Seattle waterfront, the road followed the present-day path of Madison Street, to the corner at Twenty-Third Avenue East, from there, north on Twenty-Third to East Ward Street, west on Ward Street to Fourteenth Avenue East, and north again on Fourteenth, through a hog farm located on the present-day site of Volunteer Park. The original entrance to Lake View was located on the present-day southern boundary, behind what is now the Volunteer Park Conservatory. The eastern half of today's Lake View cemetery was acquired during the last years of the nineteenth century.

While the remains of Doc Maynard waited for a road to be built to the new cemetery, another death occurred in Seattle, that of Mrs. S.P. Smith, the mother of Judge Henry Smith, namesake for Smith's Cove, now Pier 91. Hers was the first burial to take place at Lake View, in April 1873.

Today the entrance to Lake View Cemetery is on 15th Avenue East, north of Volunteer Park on Seattle's Capitol Hill. To drive, go to 10th Avenue and head east on Boston, following it until it becomes 15th Avenue. Lake View's entrance is on the right (the west side), at 1554 15th Avenue East. Bus #10 stops on 15th Avenue, just outside Lake View's gates. Hours vary depending on the season, but are generally from dawn to dusk.

How to use
this book

Begin your walking tour at the top of Lake View's highest hill, at the base of the giant red sequoia, the natural summit of Capitol Hill. The Maynard gravestones are set flush with the turf, on the tree's eastern side. It's easy to get your bearings: Look for the gray granite bench by the Whitebrook family graves. Inscribed on its sides are the words:

East The Mighty Cascades Run Free
North is The University
South, A Great Tree
West, Lies The Sound
All These Places Were Loved By Me

Sometimes, but not nearly often enough, individual plot numbers will be visible on the bottom edge of the flat markers set flush with the turf.

Follow directions in the italic type preceeding each pioneer and you should do just fine.

For an alphabetical index of pioneers, see the index at the back of the book. For a list of lot numbers with names of their occupants, see pages 110-112. The map in the back of the book shows Lake View's layout and is useful for finding specific graves.

Good luck and happy hunting.

BEGIN your walking tour at the top of Lake View's highest hill, the natural summit of Capitol Hill. The Maynard gravestones at the base of the giant red sequoia are set flush with the turf, on the tree's eastern side.

In the spring of 1906, Catherine Maynard was photographed sitting on the stone balustrade surrounding her husband's elaborate grave site. Today the Maynard gravestones lie flat at the base of the giant sequoia planted when Catherine died, a testament to the impermanence of monuments of stone, and the enduring forces of nature.

DOCTOR DAVID SWINSON MAYNARD

1808 - 1873

LOT 211

Doctor David Maynard lived his entire life with the unshakable belief that whatever he won on the next roll of the dice would be better than what he had lost on the last. It rarely played out that way, but it never stopped him from trying. He spent twenty-one years in Seattle, and no pioneer ever crowded more highs and lows into one life.

Born in Vermont, he earned the title of doctor after four years of study and an apprenticeship with a local physician. On the rebound from a failed romance, he married Lydia A. Rickey in 1828 and left Vermont to make a home in the then-new city of Cleveland on the shores of Lake Erie. (Present-day Seattleites may be surprised to learn that Doc Maynard's plan for Seattle was patterned after Cleveland.)

He prospered in Cleveland, but in a pattern that would follow him all his life, lost it all, made another fortune, and lost the second one too. In 1850 he decided to migrate to California. He departed on April 9, leaving behind Lydia, a failed marriage and two grown children.

On the Oregon Trail he met the woman who would become the second Mrs. David Maynard, Mrs. Catherine Troutman Simmons Broshears. After Catherine's husband died on the trail, Doc Maynard took over her care and drove her wagon for the rest of the trip. They stayed together for the next twenty-three years.

They arrived in Olympia, Oregon Territory, in the fall of 1850. Catherine moved into the home of her brother, "Big Mike" Simmons. Broke and encumbered with a wife in Ohio, Doc Maynard set about clearing away the obstacles in the way of marrying Catherine. He spent the winter and spring of 1851 in Olympia, chopping wood to sell to ships that intermittently arrived from San

DAVID S MAYNARD MD

Born in Vermont

MARCH 13 1873

65 YEARS

Francisco. With the proceeds, he opened a general store in Olympia, much to the annoyance of his competitor and future brother-in-law, Big Mike Simmons. At this time, Doc Maynard made the acquaintance of Sealth, the chief of the Duwamp-ish tribes to the north.

By the spring of 1852, Doc Maynard had a new scheme—to pack barrels of salted salmon and sell them to the San Francisco market. His friend Sealth told him of good fishing waters at the new settlement of Duwamps, as Seattle was then known. Maynard packed up his store and paddled north in Sealth's canoe, arriving in Duwamps on March 31, 1852.

His enterprise on the behalf of the settlement has become the stuff of legends.

The first thing he did was ditch the name "Duwamps" for the more eponymous "Seattle" in honor of his friend Sealth. Maynard started the first two commercial businesses in the settlement. The first, a general store called The Seattle Ex-change, was located on the present-day First Avenue South; the second was his salmon packing operation. Neither venture was a success, but Doc Maynard moved too fast for his failures to catch up with him. For the first twenty years of Seattle's existence, nearly all the commercial business was located on Doc Maynard's donation claim.

The Indian attack of January 26, 1856, stalled the development of Seattle and nearly bankrupted Doc Maynard. He decided to be a farmer and on July 11, 1857, traded 260 unplatted acres of Seattle for 320 acres of farmland at Alki. By 1861, he was back in Seattle, opening a hospital in The Felker House at First Avenue and Jackson Street.

In 1872, the first Mrs. Maynard arrived to claim her half of the land the doctor had claimed in 1852. He had sworn out an affidavit that she was dead. With no embarrassment whatsoever, Doc and the second Mrs. Maynard met her as she stepped off the boat at Yesler's Wharf. He then escorted the two Mrs. Maynards up the street to the amazement of the town. The three of them lived together, apparently in harmony, for months, to the amusement and wonder of the town.

By 1873, Doc's fondness for whiskey, his surplus of wives, and the ongoing litigation involving his dubious land claims had taken a toll on his health. On March 7, 1873, he diagnosed his own condition as terminal and ordered the construction of his coffin, giving explicit instructions as to how he wanted it made. He died one week later, on the evening of March 13, 1873.

Death ends a life, but not litigation. The eastern half of Doc Maynard's original land claim was in and out of the courts for the next forty years, well into the twentieth century. The lack of clear title to the land served to depress land values in the area south of Yesler and east of Seventh Avenue South. Seattle grew to the north, onto the claim of Arthur A. Denny, allowing Denny to harvest the rewards of growth, and eventually be proclaimed the father of Seattle.

Doctor David S. Maynard is credited with one more first: That is the first to be buried in Lake View Cemetery. It's not true. Mrs. S.P. Smith was the first. Her body was carried by covered wagon and was buried in lot 199 in April 1873. But then, Doc Maynard would be the last to quibble with the truth when legend was more picturesque.

*THE inscription on Catherine Maynard's stone
commemorates her role as one of Seattle's founders.
"She Did What She Could" is from the Gospel of
Saint Mark and has been a popular epitaph for
women for more than a thousand years.*

CATHERINE TROUTMAN MAYNARD

1816 – 1906

LOT 211

The study of pioneer women can be very
frustrating because so little was recorded about
them. Two early historians of Seattle, Clarence
Bagley and Cornelius Hanford, gave pioneer women only passing reference, and, when mentioned,
it was usually as wives and mothers. The individual
personalities of the pioneer women become fuzzy
and obscure. Luckily, one whose story has survived
to give a vivid portrait of pioneer life is the second
wife of Doctor David S. Maynard, Catherine
Troutman Simmons Broshears Maynard.

She was born on her father's plantation in
Kentucky on July 19, 1816, one of twenty children
of her father's two marriages. When she was fifteen
the family migrated to Pike County, Illinois, and at
the age of sixteen she married Israel Broshears.
Catherine lived the life of an Ohio farmer's wife
until 1850, when her entire extended family
decided to join the migration to the Pacific coast.

The scourge of the Oregon Trail was cholera,
and in the first week of June 1850, cholera caught
up with their party near Fort Kearney, Kansas.
Catherine's mother, husband, and five brothers,
sisters and in-laws died within a week. Doctor

David S. Maynard, who was ten miles farther west on the trail, heard of their trouble and rode back to administer what aid he could. He was too late to do more than help bury the dead. Before she died, Catherine's mother extracted a promise from him to look after her daughter, and Doctor Maynard threw in his lot with the widow Broshears. The union lasted the rest of his life, although it is questionable as to who looked after whom.

The couple continued west on the Oregon Trail, arriving at The Dalles, Oregon Territory, on September 16, 1850. They headed north to Olympia, where Doc Maynard successfully delivered Catherine to the home of her brother, Colonel "Big Mike" Simmons, a pioneer of 1845. Big Mike thanked the doctor for escorting his sister across the continent, but made it clear that, since Doc was a married man, he was not welcome as a suitor for Catherine.

To clear the way for his marriage, Doc Maynard quickly obtained a legislative divorce from his wife in Ohio and on January 15, 1853, he and Catherine were married.

For the next twenty years, Catherine followed the doctor through his ups and downs. She served as his nurse when he doctored, traveled with him to California, and lived with him at Port Madison while he served as Indian agent during the Indian Wars of 1855-1856. Legend has it that before the January 26, 1856, Indian attack on Seattle, Catherine crossed Puget Sound in a fierce storm to warn the town of the impending attack.

Catherine put up with the doctor's wheeler-dealer ways, even to the point of extending her hospitality to his first wife when she showed up to claim her half of Doc's original homestead claim.

Doc Maynard's habit of shaving the truth finally caught up with him, and when he died, Catherine was left destitute. Although she was legally entitled to twelve-and-a-half percent of Doc's original claim, his affairs were not settled until after she died, forcing her to sell her few remaining assets to survive. For a few years following his death, she kept a reading room at her home on the east side of First Avenue South, between Main and Jackson Streets. Then, for the next twenty years, Catherine lived alternately at Medical Lake, near Ellensburg, and in Seattle, regularly riding horseback across the Cascades until she was eighty. At the age of ninety, she succumbed to a chill and passed away on the evening of October 20, 1906.

Her immense funeral was held on October 23 at the First Christian Church on the corner of Olive Street and Broadway, attended by all the surviving pioneers and five hundred others. She was buried next to her husband at the top of Lake View's highest hill.

CATHERINE TROUTMAN
MAYNARD

One of the founders of Seattle

JULY 18, 1816
OCT. 20, 1906

SHE DID WHAT SHE COULD

FROM the Maynard grave sites, proceed south to the second roadway you come to. On your way, note the white Carrara marble gravestone, set flush with the turf, of the Pontius family, the namesakes for Pontius Avenue.

REZIN W. PONTIUS

unknown

LOT 175

The Pontius family and its progenitor, Rezin W. Pontius, undoubtedly did more to change the face of Seattle than any other pioneer family, albeit indirectly.

Rambling and ramshackle, Seattle in the 1880s was a frontier city built almost entirely of wood—even the streets were planked with wood timbers. The city had been slow to grow, but by the mid-1880s was booming as railroads brought more people west. During the exceptionally dry, hot spring of 1889, the city baked in the sun.

On June 6, 1889, in the basement of the Pontius Building, which was located on the southwest corner of First Avenue and Madison Street, a carpenter's glue pot boiled over and ignited the floor of the building. The fire spread through the city and didn't end until early the next day. Every building west of Third Avenue and south of Spring Street—all the way to Elliott Bay— lay in ashes, smoldering in the morning air.

The Great Seattle Fire was an urban planner's dream come true. It gave the city the opportunity to realign the one-half-block discrepancy between Doc Maynard's and Arthur Denny's original conflicting street plats. First Avenue was turned

south at Cherry Street to cut across the corner of
Henry Yesler's property and aligned with First
Avenue South at Yesler Way. Henry Yesler cleared
one hundred fifty thousand dollars in the deal by
holding the city up for ransom for the coveted
right-of-way.

Robert Moran, the mechanically inclined
mayor, and R. H. Thompson, the civil engineer
whose great dream was to pull Seattle out of the
pit it had dug itself into, led the efforts to rebuild
the city in brick and stone. Halfway through,
Thompson decided to raise the level of the street
grade by fourteen feet at First and Yesler and
rebuilt the city's sewers above the level of high
tide so they would no longer run backward with
incoming tides. Today's underground Seattle is the
legacy of that midstream change of plans.

LOOK to the southeast for a large gray granite column topped by a partially-draped urn and surrounding pedestal of one of the many Kinnear family grave sites at Lake View. Generally, these large Victorian grave monuments are set on a base with three rises, which represent the Christian virtues of faith, hope and charity. Family members' graves surround the monument.

GEORGE KINNEAR

1836 - 1912

LOT 169

While serving with the Union forces during the Civil War, George Kinnear faithfully sent his pay home every month to his mother. At the end of the conflict, his mother gave him the entire amount. It was a nest egg to get him started in Seattle real estate.

During a visit to Seattle in 1874, George Kinnear bought acreage on the southern slope of Queen Anne Hill. In 1878 he returned with his mother and brothers to make Seattle his home. Recognizing the necessity of transportation to the east, he spent the next two years building a wagon road over Snoqualmie Pass. In 1885-1886, George Kinnear was a leader of a group that supported local law enforcement authorities during the anti-Chinese agitation that boiled over onto the streets of Pioneer Square.

In 1887, the Kinnears gave the City of Seattle fourteen wooded acres on the southern slope of Queen Anne Hill, today's Kinnear Park.

FOR an interesting side trip, proceed south and stop at the second road you come to. To the left, marked on your map as plot number one, is the original entrance to Lake View. On the road in front of the Bremer monument is a tall white Carrara obelisk, the grave of Phillip H. Lewis (lot 110). To the west is the family grave site of Richard Achilles Ballinger.

RICHARD ACHILLES BALLINGER

1858 - 1922

LOT 31

The life and career of Richard Achilles Ballinger is a testament to the values of hard work, perseverance, and a personal acquaintanceship with at least four presidents of the United States.

He was born in Boonesboro, Iowa, on July 9, 1858. His father, a Richard also, had worked in Abraham Lincoln's Springfield, Illinois, law office. Richard Jr. graduated from Williams College, where he was a classmate of James Garfield, the twentieth president of the United States. In 1892, Richard Ballinger arrived in Port Townsend and entered into a law practice with the brother-in-law of President Benjamin Harrison. Ballinger was elected a judge of the Superior Court of Washington in 1894, and in 1904 was elected mayor of Seattle. His government career culminated with his appointment as Secretary of the Interior under President William Taft in 1909.

*RETURN to the road by the Kinnear grave and
proceed west along the road. On the right-hand side
you will find a natural granite boulder inset with a
bronze plaque that marks the grave of Princess
Angeline, daughter of Chief Sealth. Adjacent is a tall
Victorian fantasy of a gazebo, chosen by Henry Yesler
as the gravestone for himself and his first wife, Sarah.*

PRINCESS ANGELINE

1810 – 1896

LOT 111

During the first administration of President
James Madison, a daughter was born to Chief
Sealth and his first wife at Ole Man House on
Bainbridge Island. Sealth named her Kakiisimla,
the meaning of which is unknown. She lived her
life on the shores of Puget Sound, moving with her
people as the seasons and the fishing led them to
their traditional encampment sites, from Olympia
to Whidbey Island.

Not that any white settlements existed before
1840. Until treaties with Great Britain fixed the
border between British Columbia and Oregon
Territory in 1846, the native inhabitants of Puget
Sound were subjects of the English sovereign,
governed by its local agents, the Hudson's Bay
Company.

As the daughter of Sealth, a "Hyas-Tyee" or
"high chief" of the Duwampish and allied tribes,
Angeline enjoyed a privileged status. She married
twice, first to Dokubkun, a "big" but not "high"
chief of the Duwampish, and second to Talisha,
another low-ranking Duwampish chief.

Her two known children, daughters, both married white men. The elder, Mamie (or Mary) married William DeShaw. Their second daughter, Chewatum (or Betsy) was one of the saddest stories of early pioneer life.

In 1851, Betsy was sold by her stepfather to one of the two Joe Fosters of pioneer Puget Sound. Betsy didn't want to live with him and ran away several times, but Foster always brought her back. In 1853 they had a son, also named Joe Foster. Betsy continued to be unhappy with Joe Sr., and in the summer of 1854, following an argument with him, she hung herself with a red bandana in their Seattle waterfront cabin. The young Joe Foster despised his father and was brought up by his mother's people. He was a source of sorrow and comfort to Angeline for the rest of her days.

When Doc Maynard and his soon-to-be-wife Catherine settled in Seattle in 1852, Angeline was known as Kickisomlo-Cud, the widow of Dokub-kun, or Cud. Catherine, who knew Sealth and his daughter well, said: "You are far too handsome a woman to carry a name like that. I hereby christen you 'Angeline,'" and Princess Angeline she was for the rest of her days.

The Princess worked as a washerwoman for many of the pioneer white families and held court on the streets of the emerging town. Although Angeline never left Puget Sound, in later years, souvenir trinkets and photographs showing her bent and withered with age were sold up and down the Pacific coast.

Angeline's last ten years were spent living in a shack built by Henry Yesler, west of what is now the Pike Place Market. A scrupulously moral woman, Angeline frowned at the impertinent pioneer white child who asked in her presence: "Does Angeline know about God?" She replied in Chinook jargon: "You tell that girl I know God sees me all the time. I might lie or steal and you would never know, but God would see me do it."

She died on May 30, 1896, and at her request was laid to rest in the burial ground of her white friends. Her funeral was held at Our Lady of the Good Help Church and conducted by Father F.X. Prefontaine. Like her father, Sealth, Angeline had been baptized by Catholic priests in the 1840s. Her sole survivor was her grandson, Joe Foster.

At Lake View, Angeline was laid to rest in an Indian canoe, covered with a red shawl. Mrs. Catherine Maynard, the woman who had named her Princess Angeline nearly forty years before, stood at the head of the grave and spoke a few words of encouragement to young Joe Foster before tossing a bough of cedar into the grave.

The inscription on Angeline's gravestone, telling the story of her warning the pioneers of the impending Indian attack of January 26, 1856, is one of the most popular and persistent legends of pioneer Seattle. Alas, it is almost certainly untrue.

NEXT to Princess Angeline's stone is the monument for Henry Yesler and his wife, Sarah. The formal monument, which was a stock mail-order item, overlooks three large marble slabs for the graves of Henry and his two wives.

HENRY YESLER
1807 - 1892
LOT 111

Considering all that Henry Yesler had to start with, it's amazing he didn't end up a truly wealthy man. After all, he had a sawmill, he had timber, and he had capital to get him started. But when it came to marshaling his forces, Henry Yesler didn't have a clue.

He arrived in Seattle in October 1852, looking for a site where he could build a steam-powered sawmill, the first on Puget Sound. To give Yesler waterfront property for his mill, Doc Maynard moved his claim-stakes on the Seattle waterfront and Arthur Denny moved Carson Boren's. (Carson, Denny's brother-in-law, was out of town at the time. When he returned, he found he no longer had any waterfront property.) Having secured the land he wanted, Henry Yesler took off for San Francisco to buy mill machinery. He returned in February 1853, and the following month, he opened his mill on the Seattle waterfront at the present-day intersection of First Avenue and Yesler Way.

A steam-powered sawmill on Puget Sound in 1853 should have been a sure-fire money-making machine, but somehow, under Henry Yesler, it wasn't. He leased the mill to other operators while he and his wife, Sarah, lived on borrowed money, paying it back at interest rates of up to twenty-five percent. Seattle's first minister, the Rev. David Blaine, was the first to extend money to Yesler, loaning him two hundred dollars at fifteen percent interest in 1854.

For the next fifteen years, until the 1870s, Yesler's Mill, Yesler's Cookhouse and Yesler's Wharf were the centers of town activities. Henry Yesler was the richest man in town, but always teetered on the edge of bankruptcy. The first two known photographs of Seattle are of the Yeslers, standing in front of their original home on the northeast corner of First Avenue and James Street, the present site of the Pioneer Building. The Yeslers themselves were a happy couple and loved to dance. At town social events, they were the first to arrive and the last to leave. Henry even built Yesler's Pavilion, a new, bigger dance hall, at First and Cherry, when the town outgrew its first ballroom, Charlie Plummer's Snoqualmie Hall.

With the arrival in 1877 of Henry Yesler's capable nephew, James Lowman, the Yesler property began to be managed in a business-like manner, leaving Henry the money and leisure to do what he did really well: be the town's resident crusty, colorful old codger.

In 1883, Henry Yesler cut down his fruit orchard, and he and Sarah built themselves a huge ungainly wood mansion. Sarah died in August 1887, and shortly thereafter Henry scandalized the town by bringing his second cousin, twenty-three-year-old Minnie Gagle, to live with him. He married her in 1889. The second Mrs. Yesler was "not received" by what amounted to Seattle society, and after Henry Yesler's death in 1892, Minnie fought it out with his heirs and the City of

Seattle for her share of the estate. Minnie Gagle Yesler left the mansion, and Seattle, in 1899.

Henry Yesler planned his grave site here at Lake View to include both of his wives. The second Mrs. Yesler didn't see things quite that way, and declined. The third grave at the Yesler grave site remains empty.

AFTER viewing the Yesler grave sites, proceed north for a hundred feet. Surrounding you will be monuments and markers for some of the most prominent names in nineteenth and early twentieth century Seattle. These were very desirable grave sites, and amount to a sort of Beverly Hills of Lake View.

A squat granite obelisk still possessing some of its original chain fencing marks the grave of Hillory Butler and his wife, Catharine. Most of the large family grave sites in this area contained their own fences, made of chain or cast iron, making ground maintenance very difficult. Most have long since disintegrated or been removed.

HILLORY BUTLER

1817 - 1896

Lot 147

Hillory Butler, a member of the Bethel Party, crossed the Oregon Trail and arrived at Puget Sound in 1853. He and Dexter Horton, George Frye, Thomas Mercer and others comprise the second party of immigrants to lay claim to the present-day city of Seattle. A courtly gentleman from a fine old Virginia family, his speech and behavior made him the automatic target of pioneer humor.

During the winter of 1855-1856, when tensions with the Native Americans were about to erupt into warfare, the settlers of Seattle lived on tenterhooks, alert for sounds signaling the conflict they all dreaded. There were many late-night false alarms when all the village leapt from their beds and raced pell-mell to Fort Decatur, the fortified blockhouse at the foot of Cherry Street. During one late-night sprint, Hillory Butler and Ursula

McConna, George's widow, started out neck and
neck. According to the story, the fleet-footed
widow soon outpaced him, leaving Mr. Butler
bleating in the dark, "Wait for me! Wait for me!"
Another version has Hillory smartly outrunning
the widow McConna and his own wife in the race
to the blockhouse, leaving both of them to cry,
"Wait for me!" In this version, Hillory didn't stop
until well inside the doors of Fort Decatur.

On the morning of the actual battle, January 26, 1856, Hillory beat his previous personal-best time in the run to the blockhouse, and made a fashion statement by arriving wearing his wife's red flannel petticoat.

In spite of his less-than-glorious beginnings, Hillory Butler was a generous and productive member of the pioneer community for more than forty years. He built the Butler Hotel at the northwest corner of Second and James Street, petitioned the Grand Lodge of Free Masons to organize a Seattle chapter in 1860, and was instrumental in erecting a permanent memorial at the grave of Chief Sealth at Port Madison.

FROM the Butler grave site, turn to the east and walk about twenty paces. Look for the flat concrete markers of the Prosch family lying in the ground.

THOMAS PROSCH

1850 -1915

LOT 164

Thomas Prosch journeyed north from Steilacoom to attend Seattle's clamless "Grand Clam Bake" of July 22, 1859, along with many other Puget Sound residents. Unimpressed, he remarked afterward to his friend, Clarence Bagley, that Seattle was not, nor ever would be, the equal of Steilacoom, then a teaming town of fifteen hundred. He eventually changed his mind. Both Prosch and Bagley went on to become historians of Seattle.

Thomas's father, Charles Prosch, was a pioneer newspaper publisher on Puget Sound and editor of the *Puget Sound Herald*. In 1858, Charles Prosch wrote an editorial on the need of wives for the surplus of bachelors on Puget Sound. The article inspired Asa Mercer to import two cargos of unmarried women, called "The Mercer Girls," to Seattle —but that's another story.

Prosch became editor of the *Seattle Post-Intelligencer* in 1885. He wrote, in longhand, a comprehensive chronological history of Seattle, and biographies of both Doc Maynard and Catherine Troutman Maynard. It was Thomas Prosch who planted the giant redwood tree that grows on the grave of Catherine Maynard at Lake View's highest point.

TEN yards to the east of the Prosch family graves, look for a black granite monument shaped like a mushroom.

WILLIAM GUTHRIE LATIMER

1833 - 1898

LOT 165

Of the half dozen or so who can lay claim to being the first to settle on the land above Elliott Bay, the case for William Guthrie Latimer holding the title is as good as any, and better than most.

Born in Tennessee, he was the youngest brother of Sarah Latimer Boren Denny, mother of the Borens and the second wife of John Denny Sr. Thus, Latimer was an uncle from both sides to the entire Denny-Boren clan.

William Latimer built a small hut near the present-day intersection of Second Avenue and Columbia Street, where he lived in the summer of 1850. When the Dennys and Borens began building cabins in the spring of 1852, the remains of the hut were still visible and were noted by the later pioneers. Strangely, none of the books written by the Dennys or their descendants mentions that their double-uncle had been here before their arrival in 1851.

Latimer crossed the Cascades in the spring of 1850, possibly the first white person to travel across Snoqualmie Pass. At some point in the fall of 1850, he left Elliott Bay bound for Portland, Oregon Territory.

He returned to Seattle in 1852, and again in 1853, on one occasion hitching a ride to Seattle from Olympia in Doc Maynard's canoe. William Latimer owned the small, one-story building where the Rev. David Blaine preached his first sermon in Seattle in December 1853. He offered it rent-free to Blaine for use as a temporary church.

At this point William Guthrie Latimer disappeared from Seattle records. In 1882 he resurfaced as a wealthy real estate developer.

The only other white man known to have lived on Elliott Bay in the summer of 1850 was John Holgate (see page 98). The presence of William Guthrie Latimer on Elliott Bay at the same time raises many unanswered questions regarding the arrival of his relations, the Dennys and the Borens, in 1851 and how much information they had about the area.

PROCEED north and stop at the first road, by the large grave site of the Joe Foster family. The sides of the Foster family monument and the individual gravestones are inscribed with verse. This was very expensive, as all lettering was chiseled by hand. Nowadays, this work is done by machines.

JOE FOSTER

1828 - 1911

LOT 180

In pioneer Seattle and King County there were two different men named Joe Foster who were not related. One, a pioneer of 1852, was a solid, upstanding member of the pioneer community who helped to defend Fort Decatur during the Indian conflict of 1855-1856, and served with distinction in the Territorial Legislature.

The second Joe Foster was a liar, a thief and a wife beater (the husband of Princess Angeline, whose son was also a Joe Foster), who later came to a violent end.

The large family grave site here at Lake View is that of the "good" Joe Foster, surrounded by his wife and children.

ADJACENT to the roadway, encased under pink granite slabs, are the graves of Moses R. Maddocks and his family.

MOSES R. MADDOCKS
1833 – 1919
LOT 178

Captain Leonard Felker built Seattle's first hotel in 1853. Named after himself, The Felker House stood near the present-day intersection of First Avenue South and Jackson Street.

By 1864, Seattle was ready for a new "grand hotel" and Moses R. Maddocks built it on the triangular lot formed by James Street, Yesler Way and Second Avenue. Before the creation of Pioneer Square in 1889, the town square was one-half block to the east on Occidental Place. Maddocks' hotel, the Occidental Hotel, was the first of three hotels, each grander than its predecessor, to occupy the site.

Soon after his Occidental Hotel opened in 1864, Maddocks sold a one-third interest in it to John Collins, a Puget Sound newcomer. Collins bought the remaining interest in 1867. Maddocks continued to keep a drugstore on Front Street, now First Avenue, north of Yesler Way. The second Occidental Hotel, which had replaced the first on the original site, was destroyed in the Great Seattle Fire of June 6, 1889.

The third Occidental Hotel, renamed The Seattle Hotel, was demolished in the early 1960s to make room for the site's current structure, "The sinking ship garage." This concrete structure was so out of character with the historic buildings in the area that it galvanized the forces of historic preservation in Seattle's Pioneer Square, which led to the establishment of the Pioneer Square Historic Development Association in 1960 to preserve the area's buildings.

WEST of the Maddocks' grave is an enormous gray granite obelisk and surrounding pedestal marking the grave site of pioneer banker Dexter Horton and his three wives. Directly west, in the Smith family plot, is the grave of pioneer H. H. Tobin, whose death is the earliest to be marked in stone at Lake View.

DEXTER HORTON
1825 - 1904
LOT 181

Dexter Horton arrived in Seattle in April 1853, having come across the Oregon Trail as a member of the Bethel Party the year before. His arrival at Puget Sound marked the lowest point of his life. Broke and in poor health, he had nowhere to go but up. Over the years he acquired the greatest wealth of all the pioneer founders of Seattle.

He first worked for two dollars and fifty cents a day grubbing out stumps on William Bell's claim in Belltown. In the fall of 1853, Dexter and his wife, Hannah, a sister of William Shoudy, took over the operation of the cookhouse at William Renton's sawmill in Port Gamble. Nine months later they returned to Seattle in good health and with eleven hundred dollars in gold.

Like nearly all the men of pioneer Seattle, Dexter went to work at Henry Yesler's sawmill on the Seattle waterfront. Hannah ran the cookhouse. The building, a rough-hewn log house at the foot of Yesler's Wharf, became the center of pioneer Seattle social life.

In 1854, with partners David Phillips and Arthur Denny, Dexter operated a general store on

Commercial Street, now known as First Avenue South. It was here he got his start in banking. Early-day loggers and sailors around Puget Sound would ask Horton to hold sums of money for them. He kept the money in individual bags with the owner's name written on them, buried in the depths of his store's coffee barrel. When a depositor wanted to make a withdrawal, Horton would fish around in the barrel until he found the correct bag, write down the amount withdrawn, and rebury the balance. For years, much of the gold coin and currency in use on Puget Sound was redolent with the smell of coffee.

At one point Dexter Horton bought a used safe for his customers' money. When the safe arrived he discovered it had no back. Horton solved the problem by pushing the back of the safe against a wall and no one was ever the wiser.

In 1870, Horton and David Phillips, his partner in the store, began banking in earnest. They chartered the Horton and Phillips Bank with capital of fifty thousand dollars. When Phillips died in 1872 his executor, Arthur A. Denny, became Horton's business partner under the new name of the Dexter Horton Bank. After several acquisitions and mergers the bank is now Seattle First National Bank, or Seafirst, a subsidiary of The Bank of America of California.

Hannah Shoudy Horton died in December 1871. Dexter married Caroline E. Parsons on September 30, 1873. The second Mrs. Dexter Horton died in 1878. Dexter married a third time in 1882 when he wed Arabella C. Agard. She survived him by ten years and died in 1914.

PROCEED west to the Moran family double plot on Lake View's western boundary. Along the way, at the intersection of the main road and a small side road, are the grave sites of the Piper family, William and Martha Shoudy, Judge Henry Struve and Senator John Beard.

A unique example of an eighteenth century New England style grave marker, or "stele," marks the grave site of the Piper family. In New England this type of stele was generally made of slate and carved with a "deathshead," or skull and crossbones. The use of soft white Carrara marble, which dissolves in the Pacific Northwest dampness, seems to have been a poor choice for a permanent gravestone.

ANDREW W. PIPER

1828 – 1904

LOT 184

Pioneer historian Thomas Prosch, in his brief biographical sketch of A.W. Piper, says little about the man, but rhapsodizes about a dessert called Piper's Dream Cakes: "The people of those 1870s days, to this time, think nothing of the kind...has ever approached them in excellence." Unfortunately, we will never know what it was about them that made pioneer mouths water, because when A.W. Piper died, he took the recipe with him.

The U.S. government took the Piper property on Lake Washington for the Sand Point Naval Air Station, and, in exchange, gave the Pipers property north of Shilshole, the site of the present-day Carkeek Park.

*ALONG the western border of the cemetery is the
Moran double plot, the largest in Lake View, out-
lined by partially buried granite blocks. The unusual
bronze obelisk is surrounded by many flat granite
plaques inlaid with copper for family members.
Made of welded and riveted sheets of bronze, the
monument is meant to evoke the hull of a ship, the
source of the family fortune. The obelisk is of
Egyptian origin and represents the rays of the sun.
The Victorians embraced the obelisk as a ubiquitous
grave monument.*

ROBERT MORAN

1857 - 1943

LOTS 1147-49

Robert Moran arrived in Seattle in November 1875 with exactly ten cents in his pocket
and an aptitude for mechanics. He parlayed his
assets into one of the greatest series of accomplishments in the history of Washington state.

His empire-building began in 1882 when he
and his brother, Peter, opened a small machine
shop. Burned out in the Great Seattle Fire of 1889,
he rebuilt his own business and masterminded the
city's reconstruction while serving two terms as
mayor of Seattle. He made his big leap when he
acquired several acres of tidelands south of King
Street in December 1889 and established a new
machine works and shipyard on the site. In 1898,
at the height of the Klondike Gold Rush, he designed twelve river steamers to ferry cargo and
passengers to the gold fields. The ships were built
in twelve months and he personally piloted the
convoy to Alaskan waters. Robert Moran's greatest
shipbuilding triumph occurred in 1904, when the

battleship *Nebraska*, which he had designed, was launched with great celebration on Elliott Bay.

In 1904, Moran's doctor told him that he had less than a year to live so he sold his shipyard outright for a fortune. The doctor was wrong. Moran lived another thirty-nine years in the San Juan Islands. He used the time constructively, designing everything on his estate, including the house, all the furniture and the generator— everything except the glass—and had it built in his shops. His former estate is now Orcas Island's famous Rosario Resort.

Robert Moran also designed the striking shipyard-inspired monument marking the family burial plot here at Lake View.

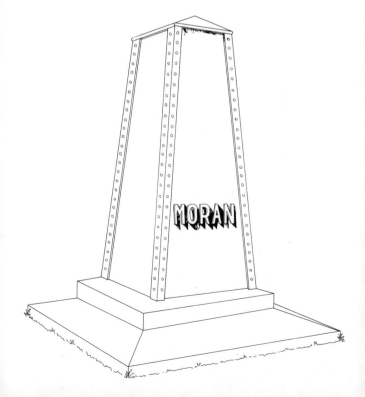

FROM the Moran family plot, return to the north-south road. Sixty feet to the northeast can be found the graves of James and Clarissa Colman.

A blue-white zinc casting, referred to in the memorial trade as white bronze, marks the Colman grave site. This type of memorial was available by mail-order through the Sears, Roebuck and Co. catalog. Colman's memorial has recently been vandalized and its top removed. Vandalism is a growing problem in cemeteries, and many of the memorials here in Lake View show the scars of defacement.

JAMES MADISON COLMAN

? - 1886

Lot 251

This James Colman was the subject of one of the most lurid criminal trials of nineteenth century Washington Territory.

On Monday morning, February 8, 1886, James M. Colman, a commissioner of King County, left his home on the eastern shore of Lake Washington to row over to Seattle. Accompanying him was a neighbor boy, William Patten. Colman's wife, Clarissa, waved goodbye from the shore.

A month later Colman and Patten's bodies were found at the south end of Mercer Island. Police arrested G. H. Miller, who had a reputation as "a desperate character," because it was known he hated Colman. However, authorities failed to gain a conviction at his trial in Seattle. Two more trials followed before Miller was finally convicted of the murders. In the meantime, Miller's daughter, Josephine, committed suicide.

On appeal, Miller's conviction was overturned by the Washington State Supreme Court. A few months before Miller's death in 1894, his son, William Miller, who had been declared insane and confined to the asylum at Steilacoom, offered to show authorities where the murder weapon had been thrown into Lake Washington.

William Miller told how he and his mother camped out on the trail from the Colman farm to Newcastle, while his father and sister Josephine did likewise on the south end of Mercer Island, lying in wait for Colman to come by. William Miller offered his testimony in exchange for his release from Steilacoom.

It was a celebrated case for years and had far-reaching repercussions. At Miller's third trial in Port Townsend, the judge made a few remarks "that reflected badly on Sheriff McGraw," who had mishandled the case during his investigation. The insults started a political feud that resulted in McGraw, who was later governor of Washington, leaving the Republican party and becoming a Democrat.

NOW walk directly north, across the road from the Dexter Horton grave site. The grave of James Osborne is under a white Carrara marble column, set on a concrete pedestal. The line proceeding due north of this site was originally a road, long since closed off and the land sold as burial sites. Many of the graves removed from The Old Seattle Cemetery in 1884 were reinterred along this road.

JAMES OSBORNE

1834 - 1881

Lot 197

No one knew if it was atonement or civic pride that caused James Osborne to leave his estate to the City of Seattle for the construction of an opera house. But he did, and the current Seattle Opera House, previously known as the Civic Auditorium, was his parting gift to Seattle, built with funds he left in trust for its construction.

He was the owner and operator of the notorious Gem Saloon, the wildest of the south-of-Yesler joints that gave Seattle the title of "Sin City on Puget Sound." One wonders what James Osborne would think of the current gentrification of the Pioneer Square district that was the home of Seattle's wild and wicked past.

*LOOK under the boughs of the giant western hem-
lock on the northeast side of James Osborne's grave
for the modest family monument of William Meyben-
bauer. Of no particular identifiable style, this stone
marks the family grave site of one of Bellevue's major
landowners. Granite squares mark individual graves.*

WILLIAM MEYDENBAUER
1832 - 1906
LOT 218

The namesake of Lake Washington's
Meydenbauer Bay and Bellevue's Meydenbauer
Creek and Park had another claim to fame.
William Meydenbauer was the third owner of the
Eureka Bakery, a pioneer confectionery that began
the fortunes of several pioneer families.

Charles Terry started the Eureka Bakery in
1864. After his death in 1867, the bakery was
acquired by George Frye, who sold it to William
Meydenbauer in 1871. The Eureka was as good as
its name and brought good luck to its owners.

FIFTY feet to the north of the Meydenbauer plot, an eight-foot white Carrara obelisk for the Wycoff family stands under the boughs of a western hemlock. Carrara marble has been mined from the mountains of Carrara, Italy, since before the time of Christ.

LOUIS WYCOFF

1830 - 1882

LOT 233

Louis Wycoff arrived in Seattle in October 1853. The first person he met was Doc Maynard, who was manfully, if not competently, trying to shoe a horse. Wycoff stopped to enjoy the doctor's efforts. Doc, who didn't enjoy being the object of mirth, finally threw down his tools and asked the stranger if he thought he could do any better. Wycoff replied that he certainly thought he could, as he happened to be a blacksmith by trade. Doc Maynard replied, "If you will take this shop and operate it, I'll sell you the land and the building for ten dollars." Wycoff pulled ten dollars from his pocket and said, "Here's the money. Give me the deed!"

Wycoff served as sheriff of Seattle for twenty years. In 1882 a mob seized two men arrested for a murder and hanged them from the maple trees on the side of Henry Yesler's home. Sheriff Wycoff, who was at home and unaware of the mob's action, was so shattered by the lynching that he died of a massive heart attack two days later.

Alongside Wycoff's grave are the graves of his wife, Ursula McConna Wycoff, and his stepdaughter, Eugenia McConna, the first white child born in Seattle.

DIRECTLY west of the Wycoff plot are the graves of Samuel Coombs and the Coombs-Watson family members, which are marked by small flat stones set flush with the turf.

SAMUEL F. COOMBS

1830 – 1908

LOT 231

Before 1860, the political division of Seattle could be pinpointed on a map. Homes or businesses located south of Mill Street, now Yesler Way, were owned by Democrats; places north of Mill Street were owned by Whigs, or later, Republicans.

One of the businesses south of Mill Street was the notions store of Samuel Coombs, opened in 1860. He also served as postmaster and notary public. Before 1865, almost all of the business activity took place south of Mill Street, on the original claim of Doc Maynard. Soon after Lincoln was elected as the first Republican president in 1860, Seattle's business district began its northern migration onto the claim of Arthur A. Denny.

By 1870, Samuel Coombs was a hotel keeper. He named his hostelry "The Western Terminus" in anticipation of the arrival of the railroad, an event that didn't actually take place until 1887.

*FROM the Coombs-Watson graves, proceed directly
east, up the hill toward the circle road. Along your
route can be found, in lot 216, a flat gray granite
tablet set flush with the turf — the grave of Milton
Densmore.*

MILTON F. DENSMORE

1839 -1908

LOT 216

Milton Densmore arrived in Seattle in
1871, a veteran of the Army of the Potomac and a
survivor of the Battle of Gettysburg.

He was the captain of the *Linna C. Grey*, a
barge used to carry coal from the mines on the east
side of Lake Washington across to Lake Union.
The coal was off-loaded on Lake Union's northwest side to a narrow-gauge railroad that ran along
the present route of Westlake Avenue and then
across Pike Street to coal bunkers on the Seattle
waterfront.

Densmore later kept Seattle's first grocery
store at the corner of Third Avenue and Union
Street. The present-day Densmore Avenue is
named for him.

AFTER pausing at the Densmore grave site, proceed across the road to the east, toward the large white birches within the circle road. If the area to the southwest is the Beverly Hills of Lake View, then this is Bel Air. Included within this circle are the graves of many pioneers bearing some of the most prominent names in Washington Territory and early Washington state.

An enormous rusticated cross at the southern end of the circle marks the joint grave sites of John Leary and Elisha Ferry. To the left of the cross are the graves of the Learys; the Ferrys are on the right. At the turn of the century, business partners in life frequently purchased cemetery property together in order to perpetuate relations to the end of time.

JOHN LEARY

1837 - 1905

CIRCLE EE

John Leary arrived in Seattle in 1869 and was admitted to the bar association in 1871. He was involved in railroads, lumbering, politics, real estate, manufacturing, and a favorite nineteenth century legal pastime, pointless and harrassing litigation. Leary became the partner of Elisha Ferry and, at one time or another, virtually every other major capitalist of nineteenth century Seattle.

He and Henry Yesler built the Yesler-Leary Building, which stood in the middle of the present-day intersection of First Avenue and Yesler Way. Its ornate lumber mass provided a spectacular blaze for about fifty minutes during the Great Seattle Fire of June 6, 1889.

On August 21, 1892, John Leary cemented the Leary-Ferry partnership by marrying Elisha

Ferry's daughter, Eliza Ferry. They started construction of a grand house on Capitol Hill, high
above Lake Union, but John died before it was
finished. Eliza completed it and lived there until
her death. It was heavily damaged by fire in 1979
and has since been restored. Known as the Leary
Mansion, it now serves as the working office of the
Bishop of the Episcopal Diocese of Olympia.

SEPARATE headstones surrounding the cross at its base mark the graves of Leary and Ferry family members.

ELISHA P. FERRY

1825 - 1895

CIRCLE EE

John Leary and Elisha P. Ferry formed such an enduring partnership that it lasts until this day, as anyone viewing the two pioneers' joint grave site can plainly see. Both men formed partnerships with many different pioneers at various times, but the Leary-Ferry partnership had the added cement of marriage, when John Leary married Elisha Ferry's daughter, Eliza.

Elisha Ferry arrived in Puget Sound in 1869 after he was appointed Surveyor General by President U.S. Grant. When Washington became a state in 1889, Ferry became its first governor, a position that was mostly ceremonial at the time.

AFTER viewing the Leary-Ferry grave sites, continue around to the north on the west side of the circle road and stop at the ten-foot-tall variegated granite stele that marks the Shorey family burial plot. This type of grave monument was used in pre-Christian Rome. Similar examples can also be found in the ruins of classical Greece.

The inscription on the stele for Oliver and his wife, Mary, notes that he was a pioneer of 1852.

OLIVER CHADBURN SHOREY

1831 – 1900

CIRCLE M

Oliver C. Shorey was the founder of Seattle's oldest business establishment, the firm we know today as the Bonney-Watson Company.

The first mention of O. C. Shorey on Puget Sound was in 1860 on the occasion of his marriage to Mary Bonney, "one of the beautiful Bonney girls" of Pierce County. The following year they moved to Seattle, and O. C. Shorey went to work on the town's Territorial University.

The Rev. Daniel Bagley had engineered a scheme to build an enormous "university" on the land now occupied by the Four Seasons Olympic Hotel. Although of dubious legality, the project infused the village of Seattle with $30,000 of cold, hard cash. Before the Territorial Legislature caught on, the university was built and ready to use— even though there wasn't a single qualified student in the entire Washington Territory. Almost every male citizen of Seattle got a piece of the action.

Oliver Shorey hauled materials to the site and carved the Doric style capitols of the main building's fluted Ionic columns. With his wages, he opened a cabinet-making shop on the corner of Third Avenue and Cherry Street. In those early times, the local cabinet maker also built coffins when needed, and in that way, O. C. Shorey moved into the undertaking business.

In 1881, Shorey's brother-in-law, Lyman Bonney, settled in Seattle and became his partner. Eventually, Shorey sold the entire business to Bonney, who later partnered with Harry Watson to form the Bonney-Watson Company.

Because so many pioneer records were destroyed in the Great Seattle Fire, O. C. Shorey's records from his undertaking business have become an important source for historians.

NORTH of the Shorey family plot a series of gray granite tablets lying flat mark the graves of Gardner Kellogg and his family.

GARDNER KELLOGG

1839 - 1918

CIRCLE L

Gardner Kellogg, a pioneer druggist, arrived in Seattle in the spring of 1863. He built his drugstore on Mill Street, the present-day Yesler Way, where the Merchants' Cafe building now stands. Appointed postmaster under Abraham Lincoln, he ran the post office out of his drugstore.

An active leader of the pioneer community for more than forty years, he was married to Sarah, one of "the beautiful Bonney girls," a sister of Lyman Bonney.

ON the opposite side of the circle enclosure, to the east, are the graves of Henry A. Atkins and John T. Jordan, respectively the first and second mayors of Seattle. South of the Atkins/Jordan graves are the graves of Dr. Richard Fuller and his mother, the founders of the Seattle Art Museum.

HENRY A. ATKINS
1827 - 1885
CIRCLE K

There have been two incorporations of the City of Seattle. The first was in 1865, and its first elected mayor was Henry A. Atkins; he also later served one term as sheriff of Seattle.

Atkins arrived in Seattle in the fall of 1860. He and his partner, William Shoudy, who was himself mayor later, ran a general mercantile business, housed in Seattle's first brick building.

From its founding, Seattle had been operated as the personal fiefdom of its most prominent landowners, who preferred to keep it that way, thank you very much! In 1877 Henry Yesler brought suit against the City of Seattle and was able to establish that there had been no legal basis in the territorial law to establish the city. As a result, the City was forced to disincorporate.

The citizenry didn't try again until the 1880s, when the population explosion made the town ungovernable. Seattle was once again legally established. The second City of Seattle took.

AFTER viewing the sites on the east side of the circle, cross again to the west side and go down to the circle road. The recently installed granite sarcophagus of Dr. Giovanni Costigan is a type not used in Lake View for more than sixty years. Dubbed by its manu-facturers a "personal mausoleum," it was built and shipped intact from Georgia, and leveled on-site using blocks of ice. Immediately to the north are the unmarked graves of John Pike and his son, Harvey.

JOHN PIKE

Unknown

LOT 328

John Pike, one of the many members of the Bethel Party to head north, arrived in Seattle in 1858. His fellow Bethel member, the Rev. Daniel Bagley, arrived in 1860 and began finessing the construction of a grandiose "University." Pike, a handy fellow to have around, drew up the plans for the handsome buildings. He also helped clear the land and construct the buildings from his own drawings. When Arthur A. Denny platted the northern section of his claim, he named Pike Street in honor of John Pike.

John Pike's son, Harvey, took a land claim on the narrow isthmus between Lakes Union and Washington and actually started to dig a canal by hand, with pick and shovel. Eventually it became clear that it was too big a job for one man, but the present-day Lake Washington Ship Canal follows the route he started in 1869.

TURN ninety degrees to the north from the Costigan tomb and you are viewing one of Lake View's most impressive family grave sites, that of the Denny family, regarded by many as the founders of Seattle. At least four generations of the Denny family are buried here. The graves' arrangement gives a hint of the family heirarchy — notably missing are the graves of David T. Denny and his wife, Louisa Boren Denny, who are buried at Washelli Cemetery on Aurora Avenue North.

ARTHUR ARMSTRONG DENNY

1822 - 1899

LOT 342

There is some difference of opinion as to the character and personality of Arthur A. Denny. Was he in fact the pillar of pioneer Seattle that he is made out to be in many early histories of the city? Or, was he, in fact, a petty, mean-spirited, humorless man who grabbed all the credit for the founding of Seattle, and then foreclosed on the real founder, his younger brother, David T. Denny? A good case can be made for both points of view.

Historians Cornelius Hanford and Clarence Bagley portrayed him as the visionary leader of the new community, as do books written by his grand-daughters, Roberta Frye Watt and Sophie Frye Bass, and his niece, Emily Inez Denny. Roger Sale, in his 1976 book, *Seattle, Past To Present*, assigns most of the credit for the founding of Seattle to Arthur A. Denny, but he also writes, "There is no record of anyone ever having said they liked him."

Arthur Denny served with distinction in a half-dozen civic and government positions, from pioneer postmaster to legislative representative. However, the most revealing character assessment may be one made by Native Americans. In the fall of 1855, Arthur Denny was returning to Seattle from the Territorial Legislature in Olympia. He traveled by Indian canoe, paddled by two Duwampish braves. At one point in the journey, another canoe of warriors pursued Arthur's canoe. Shouting across the water, they threatened to kill Arthur Denny because he was a "Hyas-Tyee" or Great Chief of his people. Warding off the attackers, the braves paddling Arthur's canoe shouted back that he wasn't all that great.

By 1890, both Arthur and his brother, David, had achieved some wealth, mostly due to their land holdings. David risked all of his and was wiped out in the huge financial panic of 1893. Arthur, who rarely took a risk in his life, did nothing to help his brother, although he was in a position to do so. It's interesting to note that in all the books written by the Dennys and their descendants, the family has entirely closed ranks and no dirty linen was ever aired in public. Only in Emily Inez Denny's book, *Blazing The Way*, is there the brief gentle rebuke: "If he did not always do justice to others, it was the fault of his associates."

Arthur A. Denny lived out his days in his unimposing home on First Avenue between Union and University Streets, the present site of the new Seattle Art Museum. For ten years before Arthur's death in 1899, retail developers tried to talk him into selling his home with its pasture and orchard. Arthur always answered with the only attempt at real humor ever attributed to him: "But what would I do with my cow?"

PIONEER women often lived longer than their spouses and so were left to choose the family grave sites and memorials. In a competition for splendor and ostentation, Mary Boren Denny's efforts with the Denny plot would be a clear winner. The gravestones are carved from pink granite, with lettering on individual tombstones picked out in gilt. A black and white diagonally checkered marble walkway leads to the family monument, a free-standing granite column. The partially-draped urn at the column top is classical Greek, which symbolically allows the soul of the departed to ascend to the heavens.

MARY BOREN DENNY

1822 - 1910

LOT 342

In 1843 Mary A. Boren, the eldest daughter of Richard Freeman Boren and Sarah Latimer Boren, was the first of her family to marry a Denny. Seven years later, Arthur, his Denny blood itching to move west, asked her: "Mary, will you go?" and she replied; "Yes, Arthur, I'll go." She might have had second thoughts had she known she would make the trek across the continent in an increasingly advanced state of pregnancy. After 134 days on the Oregon Trail, she gave birth to her son, Rolland Denny, in Portland, Oregon Territory, on October 4, 1851.

In her later years she liked to tell the story of how her wedding gown had been stolen when their cabin was looted during the Battle of Seattle on January 26, 1856. She was always pleased to think of an Indian maiden trailing her wedding gown through the Pacific Northwest woods.

TO the right of the graves of Arthur and Mary Denny is the grave of their oldest son, Rolland, and his brother Orion.

ROLLAND DENNY

1851 – 1935

LOT 342

The oldest son of Arthur A. Denny and Mary Boren Denny, Rolland Denny was an infant at the time of the 1851 Alki landing. The local Native Americans had never seen anything quite like the blond, blue-eyed, curly-headed baby. They would click their tongues and mutter: "Acha-da, Acha-da, Memaloose, Memaloose!" (Too bad, too bad. He die soon!) They were quite wrong, however. He lived eighty-four years and was the last survivor of the original Denny-Boren landing party when he died in 1935.

ORION DENNY

1853 – 1916

LOT 342

Orion Denny, the second son of Arthur A. Denny and Mary Boren Denny, was the first white male born in Seattle, a fact he used to lord over the other pioneer children. He played up that distinction for the rest of his life. The only pioneer child who could, and did, pull rank on him was Eugenia McConna, the daughter of George and Ursula McConna, who was the FIRST white American native Seattleite, born in 1852.

ON the left side of the walkway leading to the family monument is the grave of the father of all the Dennys.

JOHN DENNY

1793 - 1875

LOT 342

The senior Denny, John Denny, was the father of all the Dennys and the stepfather of Boren women who married his sons, creating complicated family genealogy.

Born in Kentucky during George Washington's second term in office, John Denny spent virtually his entire life moving from one frontier to the next. During his long life, he helped develop five states.

At the age of nineteen, he enlisted for service with the Kentucky Mounted Volunteers, under the command of William Henry Harrison, ninth president of the United States. John Denny fought in the battle of Tippecanoe and was present at the death of the legendary Indian Chief Tecumseh. After his discharge in 1814, John Denny married Sarah Wilson of Kentucky and moved to join his brothers in Washington County, Indiana Territory. The next move, in 1834, was to Knox County, Illinois. By that time, he and Sarah had eight sons: Lewis, Alford, John Fletcher, Arthur A., James, Samuel, David T., and A.W. or Wiley.

In 1841, Sarah Wilson Denny died at the age of forty-four. Seven years later John Denny married another Sarah, Sarah Latimer Boren, a widow from Tennessee with three children: Mary, Carson and Louisa. John Denny's fifth son, Arthur A., had married Sarah's daughter, Mary, in 1843. The

Denny-Boren marrying came to an end when David T. Denny married Louisa Boren in the Arthur Denny waterfront cabin on January 23, 1853. They were married by the newly named justice of the peace, Doctor David S. Maynard.

By now, John Denny was a force in Illinois politics and served in the Illinois Legislature with Abraham Lincoln. Denny and Lincoln were among a group who broke up a quorum by leaping out of a second-story window of the Illinois statehouse.

In the spring of 1851, John Denny and family were on the move again. This time it was to be across the Oregon Trail to the Willamette Valley, Oregon Territory. The party was comprised of John and Sarah Denny, their young daughter, Loretta, and five of John Denny's sons: James, Samuel, David T., Wiley, and Arthur, with his wife and two daughters. Also included were Sarah's son, Carson Boren; his wife and daughter, Louisa Gertrude; and Sarah's unmarried daughter, Louisa Boren. David T. Denny and Louisa Boren would later unite and become the third Denny-Boren marriage.

After 134 days of travel by covered wagon, the Denny-Boren Party reached Portland, Oregon Territory. There, the party split up: Arthur and his family, David T. Denny and Louisa Boren, and the Carson Boren family moved on to Puget Sound, and landed at Alki on November 13, 1851. John Denny kept a farm at Waldo Hill, Oregon Territory, until 1859, when he too moved on to Seattle.

During his years in Seattle, John Denny was regarded as an elder statesman of the young territory and was a force in Republican politics until his death in 1875. His grave was moved here from The Old Seattle Cemetery in 1884.

TO the left of John Denny's grave is the grave of his second wife, Sarah.

SARAH LATIMER BOREN DENNY

1805 - 1888

LOT 342

The second wife of John Denny, Sarah Denny, was both paternal and maternal grandmother to the whole Denny-Boren clan.

Her first husband and the father of her three older children, Mary, Carson and Louisa, was Richard Freeman Boren, a Baptist minister from Tennessee. To support his family, Richard Boren worked as a cabinet maker. Shortly after the birth of their youngest child, he sold all of his woodworking tools and told his wife that his work was done. Two months later he was dead. His widow moved her young family to Knox County, Illinois, where the Denny-Boren marrying began. She and John Denny had one daughter, Loretta Denny.

In her later years Sarah spoke fondly of her first husband, saying that he never spoke a cross word to her. A rare biographical sketch of her appears in Emily Inez Denny's book, *Blazing The Way.*

AT the rear of the Denny family plot, resting under a considerably less impressive tombstone, lies the grave of Carson Boren. Next to Carson's is the grave of his daughter, Louisa Gertrude. The whereabouts of the grave of her brother, William Richard Boren, who may or may not be Carson Boren's son, is unknown.

CARSON BOREN

1824 - 1912

LOT 342

The Denny-Boren family genealogy is so complicated the average reader may need graph paper in order to keep the relationships clear (check back to John Denny, page 60, if in doubt). But all this background family history is necessary if one is to understand the shadowy figures of Mr. and Mrs. Carson Boren, the most enigmatic of the five couples who made the first land claims above Elliott Bay.

Carson Boren and his wife, Mary, and young daughter, Gertrude, came across the Oregon Trail with the rest of the Denny-Boren Party in the spring and summer of 1851, and landed at Alki on November 13, 1851. After spending the winter at Alki with his wife and child and Denny in-laws, Carson, William Bell and Arthur Denny made claims to the land comprising present-day downtown Seattle on the other side of Elliott Bay. Bell's claim was to the north, Arthur's in the center, and Boren's to the south. All three made claims of three hundred twenty acres allowed to a married couple, and each shared an equal amount of waterfront. The Carson Borens built the town's first cabin on the northwest corner of Second

Avenue and Cherry Street, the present site of the
Hoge Building.

Now, the *really* interesting stuff begins. On
March 23, 1852, Carson Boren and his brother-
in-law, David T. Denny, sailed to Olympia on
board the schooner *Exact*, en route to the Willamette Valley to pick up livestock left to winter over.
On March 31, 1852, Arthur Denny moved Carson
Boren's claim-stakes to make room for the settlement's newest arrivals, Dr. David S. Maynard and
his soon-to-be-wife, Mrs. Catherine Broshears. In
October, Arthur moved his brother-in-law's claim-
stakes again, this time to make room for Henry
Yesler and his sawmill. By now, Carson had no
water frontage but still owned most of the hill now
occupied by downtown Seattle.

In the many books written by the Dennys
and their descendants, the family is silent regarding Arthur's pioneer claim-jumping. By their
accounts, Carson Boren was a gentle and easy-
going man who loved the fields and forests, far
from the habitations of man.

His problem was a bad marriage. Mary
Boren was a shrew of a woman and after their
son's birth, on October 4, 1854, their marriage
failed completely. In April 1855, Carson and Mary
Boren sold the west half of their claim to Edward
Lander and Charles Terry for five hundred dollars,
and agreed to go their separate ways. The proceeds
of the sale were used to finance Mary Boren's return to "The States."

For the next sixty years, Carson Boren was a
shadow figure in the development of Seattle, remembered fondly by all the pioneer children as
"Uncle Dobbins." His son and daughter, the best
looking of all the pioneer children, were brought
up in households of his Denny relations.

Carson Boren adored his children, and when William Richard Boren died in 1899 and Louisa Gertrude died in June 1912, Carson lost the lights of his life.

He was the last male survivor of the adults who landed at Alki when he passed away on August 19, 1912, at the age of eighty-eight.

*FORTY feet northwest of the Denny plot lie the
toe-to-toe grave sites of Lyman Walter Bonney and
his partner, Harry Watson. Note the Bonney
monument, which features a solid dark gray granite
block that rests on four bronze lions' feet, claws
extended.*

LYMAN WALTER BONNEY

1843 - 1922

LOT 364

The Bonney-Watson Company lays claim
to the title of the "Oldest Commercial Establishment in Seattle," but it's a fairly tenuous grasp.
Lyman Bonney didn't enter into the history of the
city until 1881, and his last partner, Harry Watson,
in 1903. The firm that eventually became Bonney-
Watson was begun by Lyman's brother-in-law,
Oliver C. Shorey, in the 1860s.

That's not to say that the Bonneys are not an old Washington family. In fact, they are one of the oldest. The family came across the Oregon Trail from Iowa in 1852 and the following year settled in Steilacoom, one of the earliest settlements on Puget Sound. The daughters of the family were referred to as "the beautiful Bonney girls." One of them married Oliver C. Shorey, another married Gardner Kellogg, a pioneer druggist.

Lyman himself was a bit of a gadabout and didn't settle in Seattle until he was nearly forty. In the intervening years he worked in a variety of businesses in The Dalles, Portland, Silver City, San Francisco, Mexico and Tacoma. He finally settled in Seattle, where he bought into the undertaking establishment of his brother-in-law, Oliver Shorey.

A rollicking, good-natured fellow, he and Harry Watson, his partner, have chosen to spend eternity toe to toe. Their elaborate grave sites make only scant mention of their respective wives.

FROM the Bonney-Watson site, step down to the adjacent roadway and walk forty yards down the road leading west. On your right, facing west, is the gray granite obelisk marking the grave of Charles Plummer.

CHARLES PLUMMER

1822 - 1866

LOT 360

In the course of history, those who are remembered are frequently those who lived long enough for their accomplishments to become venerable. Charlie Plummer didn't become famous during his short life, but his list of accomplishments in Seattle's pioneer days was second to none.

He arrived in Seattle in the summer of 1853. By that fall he had built and opened Plummer & Chase, a general store on the northeast corner of Main and Commercial Streets, now First Avenue South. His store became a center of town activity, in part because he was Seattle's postmaster until 1860. In January 1855, he married Ellender Smith, sister of Dr. Henry Smith of Smith's Cove. Charlie built her Seattle's first grand private home on the northeast corner of Jackson Street and Occidental Avenue South. Ellender died giving birth to twins the following year.

Charlie then built a new store on the southwest corner of Main Street and Commercial, with a ballroom (Snoqualmie Hall) on its second floor. Guests from all over Puget Sound attended Seattle's first grand ball there the evening of July 22, 1859. At the rear of the store, Charlie built a wharf with an above-ground floor to supply sailing ships with fresh water. His hotel, called The Conklin Place, on the southeast corner of Main and Commercial, was the second hotel venue of Seattle's legendary Mary Ann Boyer Conklin, or "Madam Damnable."

On July 4, 1860, he rowed across Elliott Bay to the home of Doctor David S. Maynard at Alki to wed his second wife, Sarah J. Harris. Charles Plummer died at the age of forty-four, and ranked with Maynard, Terry, Yesler and Denny in importance in the early development of Seattle.

ON the south side of the road you have just walked, look for a ten-foot-tall white Carrara marble obelisk, marked with the names of Kittenger and Terry. Charles Terry's grave was moved here from The Old Seattle Cemetery in 1884 and reburied here with his wife, Mary Russell Terry, their daughter, Mary Terry Kittenger, and her family.

CHARLES C. TERRY

1830 - 1866

LOT 322

All that remains to acknowledge Charles C. Terry's contribution to Seattle is the fifteen-block-long Terry Avenue. But while he was alive, he was a dynamo, and his energy drove Seattle forward in its infancy.

Charles Terry started out promoting "New York Alki," the original settlement on West Seattle of the Dennys, Borens, Bells, Lows and Charles Terry. Lee Terry, Charles' brother, and David Denny had liked the area when they explored Elliott Bay and the Duwamish (then known as the Duwampish) in September 1851. David sent word to his brother, Arthur, in Portland, "Have examined the valley of the Duwamish River. There is room for a thousand settlers. Come at once."

Lee Terry didn't stick around long. He gave his claim over to his brother, Charles, who named it "New York Alki." In Chinook jargon, "alkee" meant "in the future" or "by and by," and the longer the word "alkee" was drawn out, the further away the future. In the case of New York Alkee, the pioneers took a very long time stretching out the word.

Seattle's first great rival for preeminence on Puget Sound was the town of New York Alkee. Between 1851 and 1855, the two settlements on opposite shores of Elliott Bay competed for new settlers in the race to build a new town. After the departure of the Low family, Charles Terry owned New York Alkee completely and dropped "New York" from the town's name. Alkee became Alki. Charles Terry was a one-man chamber of commerce, relentlessly promoting his town. He took time off to marry one of the Russell girls, Mary Jane, at Port Madison, on July 13, 1855.

In spite of all Charles' efforts on behalf of his town, by 1855 it was clear that the east side of Elliott Bay had the advantage of a deep-water harbor and eventually would overtake his town at Alki. Charles bought half of Carson Boren's original donation claim for five hundred dollars in the spring of 1855 and immediately transferred his loyalty and boosterism to Seattle.

In 1857, following the Indian attack on Seattle, Charles traded his townsite at Alki for Doc Maynard's 320 acres of unplatted Seattle and became Seattle's largest land owner.

Charles Terry promoted every possible scheme to develop Seattle. He bought the Bettman Brothers General Store in 1856 and opened the Eureka Bakery, a business that began the fortunes of several pioneer families. He also built himself a fine house at the northeast corner of Third Avenue and James Street.

Charles Terry was in a position to become a very wealthy man, but like his fellow townsmen, Charlie Plummer and Doc Maynard, he died young, at the age of thirty-six, from tuberculosis. Many early pioneers believed he had the greatest vision of all the founders of Seattle.

*THIRTY yards to the southeast, look for the large
blue-gray zinc monument marking the grave of
Thomas Mercer.*

THOMAS MERCER
1813 - 1898
LOT 292

Thomas Mercer brought so much to Seattle
that it's difficult to know where to begin. He was
one of the many members of the Bethel Wagon
Train of 1853, and arrived in Seattle in October of
that year. His horses, Tab and Charlie, were the
first team in Seattle, beloved by all the pioneer
children.

Thomas Mercer made a land claim on the
southwest shore of Lake Union, adjacent to the
northern border of David and Louisa Denny's
claim. The present-day Mercer Street marks the
southern boundary of the Mercer claim. Mercer
also brought with him five motherless daughters,
who eventually married into all the pioneer families. Between his own daughters and the two
cargoes of brides brought to Seattle by his brother,
Asa, the Mercers were responsible for a great deal
of the growth of Seattle in the 1870s, and were
second to none in supplying potential brides to
Seattle's overabundance of single men.

At the 1854 Independence Day celebration,
with Seattle's entire population gathered at his
farm for a picnic, Thomas Mercer named Lakes
Union and Washington—Lake Washington in
honor of the country's first president, and Lake
Union foretelling its future role in joining Lake
Washington to Puget Sound. The Native American

population held him in high regard, and during the Indian conflicts of 1855-1856, they spared only his and David Denny's farms. When asked why they had spared the farm, the Indians replied, "We thought Old Mercer might still want it."

Thomas Mercer had brought Dexter Horton to Seattle in 1853, and thereafter, former members of the Bethel Wagon Train straggled into Seattle for years. In 1859 Thomas Mercer married for the second time. His bride, Hester Ward of Oregon, brought her friends, the Bagleys, and her brother, D. B. Ward, all of whom made valuable contributions to the emerging town. When the Rev. Daniel Bagley, yet another member of the Bethel Party, successfully promoted Seattle's farfetched "university," Thomas Mercer and the entire male population of Seattle worked to clear the land and erect its buildings.

AFTER viewing the Mercer grave site, return to the road and proceed downhill to the west. Stop at the intersection of the north-south road. On one corner are the graves of the Stacy family and on the other, the Carkeeks. The new grave is for their daughter, Gwendolen Plestcheeff—the Princess Theodore Plestcheeff—who died in 1994 at the age of 103.

From this intersection, proceed north and continue until you come to the next road. Turn right, to the east, and proceed up the road about fifty feet to the Frye gravestones on the right.

The family enclave includes the graves of George and Catherine Frye, their children, and the graves of Virgil Bogue and George Fortson, who married into this remarkable family.

GEORGE FREDERICK FRYE

1833 - 1912

LOT 422

Few men in pioneer Seattle come across time as genial and good-natured as George Frye. He was born in Drachenburg, Germany, in 1833, and crossed the Oregon Trail in 1853 as a member of the Bethel Party. He headed west, he said, "to find a land free of Negro slavery."

Like almost all of the pioneers of Seattle, George Frye worked at Yesler's sawmill for a time, where he often took milled lumber in place of wages. He used his lumber to get started in the building business. He became the second owner of the Eureka Bakery in 1867, and continued to buy and build valuable Seattle real estate. He was pioneer Seattle's first Santa Claus and founded the first musical group on Puget Sound, The Seattle Brass Band. Like many other pioneers, he was captain of the early-day steamer, the *J.B. Libby*.

Much of George Frye's early lumber-for-wages went up in smoke in the Great Seattle Fire of June 6, 1889, including the spectacular Frye Opera House located across First Avenue from the Pontius Building, where the fire started.

He married Louisa Catherine Denny in 1860 and filled their home at Sixth and Pine with a brood of talented and artistic children. In 1910, George Frye personally supervised the construction of the Frye Hotel, which still stands at the corner of Third Avenue and Yesler Way. Theirs was Seattle's most talented pioneer family, responsible for some of Seattle's best surviving early buildings.

THE larger gray granite monument marks the graves of George and his wife, Louisa Catherine Denny Frye. The smaller stones on their graves note that they were both early pioneers.

LOUISA CATHERINE DENNY FRYE

1844 - 1924

LOT 422

The oldest child of Arthur A. and Mary Boren Denny, Catherine was seven years old when she arrived in Seattle on the morning of November 13, 1851, a member of the original group of twenty-four pioneers. That night she slept in a roofless, rain-soaked cabin and woke the next morning so stiff and sore that she formed a distaste for camping that lasted the rest of her life.

On October 25, 1860, she became the bride of George Frye, who had known her since his arrival in Seattle in 1853. They didn't make a land claim as they might have. Instead, they concentrated on buying and building Seattle real estate. Two of their daughters, Roberta Frye Watt and Sophie Frye Bass, wrote books of the pioneer history of Seattle.

Near the end of her life, Catherine Denny Frye built the splendid terra-cotta-clad Decatur Building, which stands near the original site of their home at Sixth Avenue and Pike Street.

SEVERAL members of the Frye family and their husbands and children are buried nearby.

ROBERTA FRYE WATT

1875 – 1963

LOT 422

The daughter of George Frye and Catherine Denny Frye, and a granddaughter of Arthur A. and Mary Denny, this native daughter gathered together the scrapbooks and mementoes of her parents and grandparents and wrote *The Story of Seattle*. Concerned that her book didn't contain many laughs, she once asked an elderly pioneer about the fun of pioneering. The old settler looked at her for a moment, and then responded: "It wasn't funny."

SOPHIE FRYE BASS

1866 – 1947

LOT 422

Another of the talented children of George Frye and Catherine Denny Frye, Sophie Frye Bass knew Seattle when it was a small village of less than five hundred people. Her charming book of pioneer reminiscences, *Pig-Tail Days in Old Seattle*, tells the stories of the naming of the streets of Seattle. Included are personal anecdotes of many obscure personalities involved in the founding of Seattle.

FROM the Frye grave sites, return to the east-west road and cross to its northern side. A black granite monument marks the grave of yet another claimant to the title of first Seattleite, Henry Van Asselt.

HENRY VAN ASSELT
1817 - 1902
LOT 432

Born in Holland two years after the Battle of Waterloo, Henry Van Asselt is one of the half-dozen or so who might have been Seattle's first settler. He made his land claim on the eastern banks of the Duwamish River on September 14, 1851, two months before the Denny Party arrived. Along with the family of Luther Collins and the Maple family, Van Asselt was among the first seven people to settle in the present-day city of Seattle.

Although he had a reputation as a crack shot, in June of 1851, Henry accidentally shot himself, and for years afterward he would show the scar to the local Indians, knowing their belief that a man with lead in him was invincible. It worked—no Indian ever wanted to tangle with Henry Van Asselt.

Impoverished by the Indian War of 1855-1856, he worked as a laborer in the Willamette Valley for a season to earn money to rebuild his claim. When he returned to Seattle, he went into business making curly maple furniture, delighting the pioneer wives who had tired quickly of the rustic style of interior decoration then in vogue.

FROM the Van Asselt grave site, continue east, slightly uphill. On the south side of the road, near the intersection with the road above, look for an upright monument of gray granite, marking the graves of Mr. and Mrs. Ossian Carr.

OSSIAN J. CARR

1832 - 1912

LOT 420

A pioneer of 1852, Ossian Carr was responsible for carving the fluted Ionic columns that graced the portico of the original Territorial University, now the site of the Four Seasons Olympic Hotel. The columns still stand, on the present grounds of the University of Washington. When the Territorial University opened in May 1862, Mrs. Carr was the first instructor, teaching elementary education to the pioneer children. The Carr family is related by marriage to the Holgate family.

Carr's son, Edmond, laid claim to land north of Seattle, naming it Salmon Bay on the mistaken belief that the small bay was full of salmon. The Native Americans knew better. They called it "Shul-shale," the name of the Indian tribe who used the site as a fishing camp. The marina area northwest of the campsite is now known as Shilshole. Edmond later moved to Renton.

FROM the Carr family grave site, continue east, to the intersection of the road that slopes downhill to the northwest. About fifty feet from this intersection, on the east side of the road, look for a full-length, white Carrara marble slab, set flush with the turf, and one of the best stories in Lake View.

NILS JACOB OLHM
"DUTCH NED"

1828 - 1898

LOT 470

Dutch Ned, a funny old character, was unceremoniously dumped off a ship in Seattle in the summer of 1854. He was a bit slow in his thinking due to a head injury when he was young, but earned his way in Seattle carting away the mountains of sawdust generated by Yesler's mill. He then spread it over Mill and Commercial Streets, now Yesler Way and First Avenue South, making a so-called "sawdust town." Until the late 1870s much of the town's merry-making and loitering about took place "down on the sawdust."

Although he lived in a little shack at the corner of Bellevue Avenue and Republican Street, Dutch Ned was determined not to lie in a shack in death. By scrimping and saving for years, he bought himself a plot at Lake View and built himself a grand stone-and-marble mausoleum. He would host picnics at his "little house," as he called it, and had himself photographed standing at its door.

Some of the oldtimers would tease him that when he died the undertakers would race to collect his body and he would end up buried in potter's field.

Since the dimwitted Dutchman had already paid for his own funeral and grave, this worried him. So in the last years of his life, if he had nothing important to do, he would go and sit in the parlor of the Bonney-Watson undertaking establishment and just wait.

Happily, he didn't end up in potter's field, but his "little house" deteriorated and had to be taken down in the early 1970s. Now all that remains is the white Carrara marble doorpiece, slowly crumbling in the damp Pacific Northwest winters.

Dutch Ned was fondly remembered by all the pioneer children, and remains one of the most colorful characters of the earliest days of Seattle.

*AFTER paying your respects to Dutch Ned, retrace
your steps down the road heading west, past the
Carr, Van Asselt and Frye grave sites. When you
arrive at the intersection of the north-south road,
turn right, to the north. Fifty feet ahead on your right
will be the striking red granite-clad gravestones of the
James Colman family.*

*Similar in style to the Denny-Boren plot, the
Colmans rest under elaborate red granite slabs with
raised individual tombstones.*

∼

JAMES COLMAN

1832 - 1906

LOT 459

The pioneers of Seattle possessed no end of
grand ideas for the building of a city. What they
needed more than anything else was money, and
someone who actually knew how to build a city.
Both arrived in the person of James Colman.

He came to Puget Sound in 1861 when he
bought William Renton's sawmill at Port Orchard.
For the next ten years, he enjoyed a reputation as
the best mill operator on Puget Sound. In 1872, he
leased Henry Yesler's mill in Seattle and upgraded
it to a twenty-four-hour-a-day operation.

In the late 1870s, Colman completed the
Seattle & Walla Walla Railroad to bring coal from
the Newcastle mines on the east side of Lake Washington, via Renton, to the Seattle waterfront. He
built the first two stories of the Colman Building
on First Avenue, between Columbia and Marion.
The Colman Dock, now known as Pier 52, on
Elliott Bay is still a hub of Seattle's waterfront as
Washington State ferries deliver thousands of
commuters and tourists daily.

The dock has taken its share of abuse. Over the years it has burned several times and many boats have rammed it. One boat hit so hard that the enormous clock tower at the end of the dock came crashing down into Elliott Bay. Mariners, including its present tenants, have damaged the dock when they collided with it.

FROM the Colman family plot, continue north on the road until you arrive at the large Bell mausoleum. As you walk, on your right will be Lake View's most pastoral setting, the large family grave site of Granville Haller.

GRANVILLE HALLER

1819 - 1897

LOT 496

He arrived on Puget Sound in 1853 and, operating out of a storefront in Coupeville, Whidbey Island, Granville Haller amassed a sizable fortune in lumbering, shipping, real estate and general merchandise. Seattle history buffs note that present-day Coupeville is a near twin of Seattle as it appeared in the 1850s.

Granville Haller was a nineteenth century Indian fighter, a veteran of the Florida Seminole Indian Wars and the Mexican-American War, before he came to Puget Sound. In fighting the Yakimas of Eastern Washington in 1855, however, he met his match and was forced to retreat.

In 1863, while serving with the Union forces in the Civil War, he made a few intemperate remarks about Abraham Lincoln and was dismissed from the service without a hearing. It took him sixteen years to exonerate himself and regain the title of colonel.

He retired in 1883 and built an immense wood-frame mansion known as "Castlemont" on Seattle's First Hill, at the corner of James Street and Broadway. It was the first of the many huge mansions that would adorn First Hill during its brief reign as Seattle's premier neighborhood.

*THE construction of mausoleums requires special
building techniques. Over the years several of Lake
View's mausoleums that had not been properly con-
structed deteriorated so badly that they have had to
be dismantled.*

*The Bell mausoleum has been extensively
vandalized, forcing Lake View to brick over the
original entrance.*

AUSTIN AMERICUS BELL

1854 - 1889

LOT 540

The austere Victorian mausoleum that Eva
Bell had built to memorialize her young husband
stands mute, and offers no explanation to one of
the most enigmatic stories of pre-Great Seattle Fire
days.

Austin Bell was born in Belltown on January
9, 1854, the son of William and Sarah Bell, both
members of the group of pioneers of 1851. Along
with Arthur Denny and Carson Boren, William
Bell made claim to the land above Elliott Bay in the
spring of 1852. During the Battle of Seattle on
January 26, 1856, the Bell home was looted and
burned. The family fled to California.

The senior Bells returned to Seattle in 1875,
but Austin remained in California until the death
of his father, from some "unknown and strange
malady" in 1887. By then, Seattle was a boom
town, and Austin returned to Seattle to plat and
develop his now valuable city property. His wealth
continued to multiply until one fine spring
morning in April 1889, Austin Americus Bell went

to his office, closed the door, and put a bullet through his head.

Arthur Denny wrote at the time that Austin Bell had recognized in himself the symptoms of the disease that had deranged and eventually killed his father. Two months later, on June 6, 1889, the Great Seattle Fire leveled every structure west of Third Avenue to Elliott Bay, greatly increasing the value of his intact buildings in Belltown, as the Bell plat became known.

Austin's widow, Eva Bell, finished his grand-iose dream, the five-story Bell Building, still standing on First Avenue in Belltown, and the elaborate and costly grave site here at Lake View. Late in the 1890s, after a second marriage, Eva joined him here at Lake View.

*LOOK across the road from the Bell mausoleum
toward the large beech tree for a Victorian extrava-
ganza in stone. The front, most visible side of
monument, is dedicated to Sarah M. Renton, erected
by her daughters. Wm. (abbreviated no doubt to save
money) Renton's name is inscribed less prominently on
the side.*

WILLIAM RENTON

1818 - 1905

LOTS 580-581

Captain William Renton, a pioneer of 1852
and namesake for the city of Renton, has actually
lost some of his local prominence over the years. It
used to be that the hill behind Seattle's First Hill
was called Renton Hill. Prior to that it was called,
logically, Second Hill.

(Like Adam and Eve in the Garden of Eden,
the pioneers were called upon to name everything
in sight—a daunting task that sometimes led to
banal place-names like Second Hill, or, for that
matter, First Hill.)

In 1853 William Renton built a sawmill at
Alki. It proved to be a poor site, and the following
spring he moved it to Port Orchard, where it was
one of the area's most profitable. William Renton
moved to San Francisco for a few years, but
returned to Puget Sound in 1864.

FROM the Renton grave site, return to the Bell Mausoleum, turn and face directly east, and prepare for a trip overland. Before you will stretch a long line of red granite contemporary tombstones, bearing mostly Chinese names. This is another former road, converted recently to grave sites. Many graves removed from The Old Seattle Cemetery were relocated near here, on both sides of the former roadway.

On the south side of the road in lot 506 can be found the graves of Walter Graham, a pioneer of 1856, and the graves of his two "Mercer Girl" wives. Eliza Mercer Graham was a daughter of Thomas Mercer, and Katherine Stickney Graham was a member of Asa Mercer's first cargo of Mercer Girls brides. Return to the roadway and continue east, up hill and down dale. Stop at the unmarked grave in lot number 550.

NORA JOHNS HILL

1837 - 1855

LOT 550

The death of Nora Johns Hill in 1855 was the first recorded death of a white American in Seattle, and her grave here at Lake View is her fifth grave.

Her death was just the beginning of her travels.

Her first "final resting place" was on the east side of Maynard's Point, next to a tidal lagoon, the present-day Occidental Avenue South. When Doc Maynard began developing that area, her grave was moved to the grounds of Seattle's first church, "The White Church," on the corner of Second Avenue and Columbia Street. Nora's grave at the churchyard lasted for ten years. Along with the graves of other pioneers, it was moved in 1865 to the land donated by David and Louisa Denny, then called The Old Seattle Cemetery, but now known as Denny Park.

In 1884, when The Old Seattle Cemetery was converted into Denny Park, the graves were moved again. Some graves were removed to the present-day Mt. Pleasant Cemetery, some to the Masonic Cemetery, now known as Lake View, but most were moved to the the first Washelli Cemetery, on land that is now Volunteer Park.

Like other graves in Volunteer Park, Nora Johns Hill's grave number four lasted only two years and in 1886, was moved again, to Lake View. It would seem that here, perhaps, she has found her final resting place.

Her husband, John S. Hill, captain of the stern wheeler *Ranger*, a well-known ship traveling the waters of Puget Sound in the 1850s and 1860s, eventually buried three wives here at Lake View. He himself lies in an unmarked grave at lot 56.

ACROSS the red road, slightly to the west, is a gray granite monument inscribed with the names of John and Ellen Maurer. This is also the grave site of John's father, David Maurer.

DAVID MAURER

1811 - 1873

LOT 566

The hospitality industry of Seattle owes an unacknowledged debt to David Maurer, for he was the first practitioner of that trade in Seattle.

He began serving meals in Doc Maynard's Seattle Exchange Store in January 1853. Later he had an establishment of his own across the street, where he also provided lodgings. That, and the fact that he was a drinking buddy of Doc Maynard's, is about all that is known about him.

He was briefly indicted for murder in 1854, but was quickly acquitted, in spite of having pleaded guilty to the crime. (Charles Terry whispered to him in open court: "Not guilty! Say 'not guilty,' you damn fool!")

He served as a corporal in Company A in the defense of Seattle during the Indian War of 1855-1856.

David Maurer died one month after his friend, Doc Maynard. His grave was removed from The Old Seattle Cemetery when it became a city park in 1884, but transfer records do not indicate where he was reburied. Recently his grave was discovered next to the grave of his son, John Maurer. David Maurer's grave remains unmarked.

FROM the Maurer grave, return to the red granite road and, facing east, walk about twenty yards. Look for a small concrete marker set flush with the turf on the north side of the former road.

MARY ANN BOYER CONKLIN "MADAM DAMNABLE" 1821 - 1873

LOT 552

A celebrated and mysterious character out of Seattle's pioneer past, Mary Ann may or may not have been the wife of Captain David W. Conklin, who was known as "Bull" Conklin. She certainly cohabitated with him for more than twenty years, but gave her name variously as Mary Ann Boyer or Mary Ann Conklin to the census takers of 1860, 1864 and 1870. Whatever her marital status, she was better known as "Madam Damnable."

She was born in Bucks County, Pennsylvania, in 1821. Not much is known about her until 1851, when she hooked up with Bull Conklin, the captain of a whaling ship working the waters off Alaska, then known as Russian America.

She was renowned for her nasty disposition and her absolutely filthy mouth — she could swear in five languages: English, French, Spanish, Chinese, Portuguese and a smattering of German.

At some point in 1853, Bull Conklin kicked her off his ship in Port Townsend and sailed off for Alaska. She made her way to Seattle and became the mistress of The Felker House, Seattle's first hotel.

Captain Leonard Felker had brought the house around the Horn in the hold of his brig, the *Franklin Adams*. It was a complete "house kit" and he had his crew assemble it at First Avenue South and Jackson Street on land he had purchased from Doctor David S. Maynard. It was here that Mary Ann Conklin's reputation as Seattle's foul-mouthed Madam Damnable became firmly established. Even the United States Navy gave her a wide berth. She later kept a hotel built by Charlie Plummer on the southeast corner of First and Main Street, for years called the "Conklin Place."

Roberta Frye Watt says in her book, *The Story of Seattle*, that Madam Damnable was known for her good cooking and profane language. Seattle writer Bill Speidel said she was called Madam because she ran a brothel in the upstairs of The Felker House. The author recalls bringing Bill Speidel up to Lake View to show him Mary Ann's grave. Bill looked at the gravestone, showing the date of her death as 1884, and grumbled: "That's her all right, but they got the date wrong!" He was quite right. O.C. Shorey said that Mary Ann died in 1873, and he would have known—he was the town's undertaker.

Mary Ann's grave at Lake View is her third grave. Her first grave was in The Old Seattle Cemetery.

When the time came to remove Mary Ann's grave, it was found that her remains had calcified and turned to stone. She weighed over thirteen hundred pounds! Not only that, when they opened her coffin, she was found to be smiling! (No one could remember *that* happening before.) Mary Ann's stay in the first Washelli Cemetery was a brief one. By 1886, the City had decided to make a park of the place, so all the graves were moved again.

If you notice where Mary Ann's grave is today, you will note that she is buried right next to what used to be a road. The pioneer grave diggers were reluctant to carry her remains any farther than they absolutely had to, so she is, in fact, practically in the road. This area has many graves of those peripatetic deceased pioneers, some whose demise predates Lake View Cemetery by twenty years.

*DIRECTLY east of Madam Damnable's grave are
the unmarked graves of William and Abbie Castro.*

WILLIAM CASTRO

? - 1864

LOT 552

The hard times of the pioneers are well
known, but the uglier aspects of pioneer life and
death are rarely discussed. The Castros were
victims of alcohol-induced violence, which, like
suicide, was fairly common in early pioneer history.

William Castro was pioneer of Squak, the
area we now call Issaquah. A hard-working man,
he liked to drink whiskey, but not alone. He
employed local Indians on his homestead claim
and frequently paid them with whiskey.

In the spring of 1864, he brought his
beautiful bride, Abbie, whom he worshipped, to
Washington Territory. That fall, Castro's Indian
farm workers, under the influence of whiskey he
had supplied, murdered them both as they sat
down to dinner. A friend and employee, John
Hargrove, was also killed.

Originally buried in The Old Seattle
Cemetery, the Castros were moved here in 1886.

FROM the Castros' graves, continue east until you come to the north-south roadway. On the north side of the red road, to your right, you will find the grave of John Buckley.

JOHN BUCKLEY

1798 - 1874

LOT 554

The Buckleys settled in Pierce County in the early 1850s. During the Battle of Seattle on January 26, 1856, they sought refuge inside Fort Decatur, the wooden blockhouse built at First Avenue and Cherry Street.

The Buckleys were the object of Louisa Boren Denny's scorn. Before the outbreak of hostilities, the Buckleys had belittled the need for fortifications to protect the residents and had refused to help in the fort's construction. However, once the fighting started, the Buckleys were the first ones inside the doors. Records indicate as many as twenty pioneer families lived in the blockhouse for months following the battle.

The town of Buckley, near Tacoma, is named for this pioneer family.

LOOKING to the southeast from the Buckley graves, the grand Rhodes mausoleum faces the road. To its south is the tall stele, erected by the Daughters of the Confederacy in honor of southern veterans of the American Civil War. South of this stands the Duthie family memorial, done in the style of a Greek exedra, an outdoor seating area.

From the north-south roadway, proceed to the south, turn right at the first intersection and continue uphill to the west. Near the top of the hill on your right look for the side-by-side upright monuments of James Lowman and his wife.

JAMES D. LOWMAN

1856 – 1947

LOT 437

Handsome, charming and cultivated, James D. Lowman stood in stark contrast to his uncle, the earthy Henry Yesler. James Lowman came to Seattle in 1877, after his uncle Henry had asked him to manage his wharf. He soon had Yesler's Wharf operating on sound business principles. By 1886, Lowman was handling all of his uncle's business affairs, leaving Yesler free to concentrate on what he really did best—being a wealthy, eccentric old codger.

James Lowman went on to found the firm of Lowman and Hanford, a printing and publishing firm still in business to this day. In spite of his success in business, Lowman had a knack for being in the wrong place at the wrong time. At the outbreak of World War I, Lowman and his wife were in Paris. Before that, he was in the Hotel St. Francis April 18, 1906, the morning of the Great San Francisco Earthquake and Fire.

*ON the opposite side of the road, slightly east of the
Lowman graves, is the family grave site of Cushing
Ells, a survivor of the 1836 Whitman Massacre in
Walla Walla, Washington. Large red granite tomb-
stones mark the recently vandalized grave of Judge
John J. McGilvra and his family. The small granite
obelisk nearby in lot 416 marks the grave of the
Reverend George Whitworth, namesake for Whit-
worth College in Spokane.*

JUDGE JOHN J. McGILVRA

1827 - 1903

LOT 416

In the 1870s a changing of the guard took
place. Doc Maynard, Charles Terry and Charlie
Plummer, Seattle's movers and shakers in the
1850s and 1860s, had died, leaving the field to
a new sort of Seattleite. John McGilvra, James
Colman, Thomas Burke and others represented a
new Republican majority in business and politics.

John McGilvra, appointed United States
Attorney for the Territory of Washington by
Abraham Lincoln in 1864, arrived in Seattle in
1867 and took a land claim on the western shore
of Lake Washington. He cut a road through the
woods to reach his new home, "Laurel Shade,"
a pretty white house on the lakeshore. The road
became Madison Street and his house has become
the home of the Pioneer Historical Society.

FROM the McGilvra and Whitworth grave sites, proceed southeast across the lawn and look for the two obelisks, one taller than the other, set closely together, marking the graves of the Hanford and Holgate families. Many of the graves in this plot are unmarked.

EDWARD HANFORD

1807 ~ 1884

ABIGAIL HOLGATE HANFORD

1824 ~ 1905

LOT 401

John Holgate, Abigail Holgate Hanford's older brother, was one of the two men known to have spent the summer of 1850 on Elliott Bay. He wrote enthusiastically to Abigail and her husband in Iowa about the prospects for farming on the banks of the Duwampish, as the river was then known, and urged them to come and join him in the new land. Then he went back to Iowa to lead the family west. By the time John Holgate returned to Elliott Bay, the claim he had chosen was occupied by Henry Van Asselt and Jacob Maple.

The Hanfords and the Holgates took adjacent claims south of the village of Seattle, on the western slope of Beacon Hill. After clearing the land's timber to supply Yesler's sawmill, the Hanfords planted a fruit orchard on the hill's western slope above the then-extensive tide flats. To this day, blossoms of two very old pear trees can be seen in the spring from Interstate 5 where it skirts the base of the hill. It's not possible to tell if these trees were planted by Edward and Abigail, but they are on their original claim. A plum thicket also survives on the same slope.

Warned of the impending Indian attack of January 26, 1856, the Hanfords fled to the block-house at the foot of Cherry Street. Their home and outbuildings were burned and looted, and their livestock stolen. At the end of hostilities, the Hanfords and their young son, Cornelius, returned to rebuild their farm.

When Edward Hanford platted his claim in1870 he named the streets Lander, McClellan, Stevens, Sheridan, Grant, Sherman, Sterrett and Gansevroot, after the victorious Union generals of the Civil War.

The Hanford and Holgate families are buried side by side, as they lived in life. The family plot is marked by similar gray granite monuments.

MILTON HOLGATE

1841 - 1856

LOT 401

On January 18, 1856, fifteen-year-old Milton Holgate shot and killed a man who was trying to crawl through his sister Abigail's bedroom window. The intruder was a deserter from the warship *Decatur*, then at anchor in Elliott Bay for the defense of Seattle. Eight days later, Milton himself was dead, shot between the eyes as he looked out of the door of Fort Decatur during the first moments of the Battle of Seattle.

The only other fatality of the battle was a man named Robert Wilson. A bullet shattered his neck when he stepped onto the balcony of The Felker House to get a better view of the fighting. Both men were buried on the grounds of The White Church at Second Avenue and Columbia Street. Over the course of three subsequent removals, the grave of Robert Wilson has been misplaced. His was probably one of the many unknown graves removed from what is now Denny Park in 1884.

Milton Holgate's trip was more direct: his grave was moved from the churchyard to Lake View.

THE unmarked grave of Cornelius Hanford is located with the other Hanford graves.

CORNELIUS HANFORD

1849 - 1926

LOT 401

The second son of Edward and Abigail Hanford, Cornelius was born in Iowa and and was a small boy when he came across the Oregon Trail with a large party of Hanfords and Holgates in 1852, arriving in Seattle in 1854.

The homes of both families were burned and looted during the Indian attack on Seattle, and the Hanford family fled to California, returning to Seattle in 1866.

Cornelius Hanford tried his hand at a variety of occupations in Eastern Washington before settling down to read and study law in the office of George McConna Jr., in 1873. After two years of study, he was admitted to the bar in 1875.

On the afternoon of the Great Seattle Fire he was instrumental in saving the old "Katzenjammer Castle," as the old city hall was called, and the valuable real estate records it contained. He quickly recessed court and led efforts to save the old building. (Unfortunately for Seattle history buffs, the County Building containing almost all the records historians count on was destroyed.)

Through a series of purely political appointments, Hanford attained the rank of Chief Justice of the Territory of Washington by 1889. The following year, he was appointed a federal judge for the State of Washington. For the next twenty-one years, Cornelius Hanford served on the federal bench, holding court all over the state.

But his relatively hasty education in the law proved to be the undoing of his legal career.

His nemesis showed up in 1911, in the person of Leonard W. Olson.

Olson was a naturalized American citizen, and an organizer for the International Workers of the World, then regarded as a radical labor organization. Judge Hanford had revoked Olson's citizenship on the grounds that it had been obtained by fraud. The judge reasoned that since Olson was a member of the I.W.W., he wanted to overthrow the United States constitution, and therefore was ineligible for citizenship. The United States Attorney General, George W. Wickersham, patiently explained to Judge Hanford that his ruling was really quite unconstitutional, and asked him to set it aside. The judge refused to reverse his original decision. When impeachment proceedings against him were initiated in the United States House of Representatives, Judge Hanford resigned in disgrace from the federal bench on July 22, 1912.

For the next twelve years, Cornelius Hanford wrote a comprehensive history of Seattle and environs. Published in 1924, his book is a valuable source of pioneer history. Its three volumes contain gushing profiles of Seattle's late nineteenth and early twentieth century business leaders that are valentines to capitalism and the Republican Party of Washington state.

PROCEED west from the Hanford/Holgate grave sites to the crest of the hill. The natural granite boulder, quarried from Mount Rainier, on Edmund Meany's grave is set with a bronze plaque.

EDMUND S. MEANY

1862 - 1935

LOT 380

Pioneer historian and educator, Professor Edmund S. Meany was remembered as a red-haired newsboy in Seattle of the 1870s. He went on to become one of the preeminent historians of Washington state.

One of the first graduates of the Territorial University, Edmund Meany engineered the moving of the university from its original site in downtown Seattle to its present location.

Edmund Meany married a Mercer girl—that is, a daughter of Thomas Mercer, rather than one of brother Asa's transcontinental "Mercer Girls."

A true Renaissance man, he was a writer, historian, professor, linguist, raconteur and fanatical mountain climber.

DIRECTLY east of the Meany grave in the same lot will be found the graves of Doctor Josiah Settle and family.

DOCTOR JOSIAH SETTLE

1814 - 1876

LOT 380

J osiah Settle was not the sort of minister to confine himself to preaching sermons. He had a medical practice when he arrived in Seattle in 1857, but soon went into the clothing business. In 1861, along with everyone else in Seattle, he was engaged in the construction of the Territorial University, a scheme concocted by another man of the cloth, the Rev. Daniel Bagley.

In the late 1860s the demand for timber, Seattle's chief export, dried up, and the reign of the region's second commodity, coal, began. Coal had been discovered in abundance as early as 1853, but the Duwamish Coal Company, the first chartered company in King County, lacked the capital necessary to exploit the deposits. In 1866 Dr. Josiah Settle and the Rev. George Whitworth, both men of the cloth, formed the Lake Washington Coal Company.

The Reverends Settle and Whitworth sold their fledgling coal company to outside capitalists who had the financial backing to build transportation systems to move coal from the Newcastle mines east of Lake Washington to markets in California. Coal would continue to be Seattle's chief export throughout the 1870s.

IMMEDIATELY to the east of the Meany and Settle grave sites, marked by a black granite monument flanked by two junipers, is the grave of the man most responsible for establishing the St. John's Lodge of the Order of Freemasonry in Seattle—John Webster. It was this lodge that began the Masonic Cemetery, which is now known as Lake View.

JOHN WEBSTER

1816 - 1891

LOT 379

Born in 1816 of Irish parents in Manhattan, New York, John Webster told the most fantastic stories of his experiences as a whaler in the North Atlantic. He once insisted that a gigantic whale harpooned in the mid-Atlantic had dragged his ship for fourteen days, until nautical reckoning showed the ship to be just west of Africa!

John Webster arrived at Puget Sound in 1857 and settled in Port Gamble, where he worked as a millwright and blacksmith. In 1860, along with Hillory Butler and others, he established the St. John's Lodge. The first lodge meetings were held in Yesler's Cookhouse, an informal community meeting place. Webster often traveled across Puget Sound in an Indian dugout canoe to attend lodge meetings. He served in the Territorial Legislature in 1860, and settled in Seattle in 1861, becoming the First Worshipful Master of the St. John's Lodge.

FROM the grave of Josiah Settle, return to the circle road. On the east side of the road, just below the roadway, are the most famous graves in Lake View.

BRUCE LEE
1940 - 1973

BRANDON LEE
1965 - 1993

LOT 276

Although martial arts film stars Bruce and Brandon Lee can't be called pioneers, their graves are the most heavily visited in Lake View Cemetery.

Bruce Lee is revered as the founder of the discipline of Jeet Kune Do. His cult status and fame only increased after his death from complications following surgery in 1973. Admirers from all over the world have made the pilgrimage to Lake View to leave flowers, coins, and gifts of food and incense on his grave. His son, Brandon, killed in a freak accident in 1993 while filming "The Crow," lies next to him.

The Lees' local rival for glamour is the grave of rock star Jimi Hendrix, in Greenwood Cemetery near Renton.

FROM the Lee graves, walk south and look for the blackened, free-standing column, a memorial to Captain Jefferson Davis Howell.

JEFFERSON DAVIS HOWELL

1841 - 1875

LOT 276

In the early 1870s, J.D. Howell was the captain of the steamship *The Pacific*, the first ship to sail between San Francisco and Seattle on a regular schedule. He was also the brother-in-law of Confederate President Jefferson Davis.

Considering the great distance involved, there are a number of surprisingly strong links between Puget Sound and people prominent in the American Civil War.

General George McClellan, Lincoln's timid General of the Army of the Potomac, made an attempt to survey Snoqualmie Pass in the early 1850s. William Pierce's Secretary of War, Jefferson Davis, suppressed favorable reports of the pass as a route for the proposed Northern Pacific Railroad in an effort to limit the power of the northern states and territories. Ulysses S. Grant was station-ed at Fort Vancouver and Port Townsend in the 1850s. He mentioned Seattle in letters to his wife.

John Denny, Arthur and David Denny's father, knew Abraham Lincoln well. They served together in the Illinois Legislature, and the elder Denny once visited Lincoln in The White House. Union general George Sheridan did a tour of duty at Fort Vancouver, and General George Picket, leader of Picket's Charge at the Battle of Gettysburg, was stationed at San Juan Island in 1861.

The memorial to Captain J.D. Howell at Lake View commemorates his death at sea in November 1875, when the *Pacific* collided with the *Orpheus* off Cape Flattery. Of the more than one hundred people on board both ships, there were only two survivors.

Sophie Frye Bass, in her book, *Pig-Tail Days in Old Seattle*, said that Seattle's Howell Street was named for Captain Jefferson Davis Howell.

THE last, but by no means least, stop on this tour can be found at the southeast corner of Lake View, next to the road that passes in front of the large pink granite apartment-style mausoleum.

DOROTHEA GEORGINE EMILE OHBEN "LOU GRAHAM"

1857 - 1903

LOT 926

Seattle's most successful business woman of the 1880s and 1890s was the woman known as Lou Graham. She built and operated a "Parlor House," more commonly called a brothel, at the corner of Third Avenue South and South Washington Street. Her first house burned to the ground in the Great Seattle Fire of June 6, 1889. The handsome replacement she built on the site still stands.

The late Henry Broderick, a Seattle realtor for more than fifty years, is reported to have said that more city business was conducted at Lou Graham's than at City Hall. It may be true. After all, they were only a couple of blocks apart.

Lou Graham died on a trip to San Francisco in 1903. Although many claimed to be her heirs, none were ever proven, so the proceeds from her large estate went to benefit the common schools of King County. Her grave site, in this less prominent section of Lake View, was chosen by her executor. One wonders if perhaps he was trying to distance her from her former clientele, up on the hill to the west.

LIST OF GRAVES

31	Richard Achilles Ballinger	1858 - 1922
111	Princess Angeline	1810 - 1896
111	Henry Yesler	1807 - 1892
111	Sarah Yesler	1821 - 1887
147	Hillory Butler	1817 - 1896
160	William H. Shoudy	? - 1905
164	Charles Prosch	1820 - 1913
164	Thomas Prosch	1850 - 1915
165	William Guthrie Latimer	1833 - 1898
169	George Kinnear	1836 - 1912
175	Rezin W. Pontius	? - ?
178	Moses R. Maddocks	1833 - 1919
180	Joseph Foster	1828 - 1911
181	Dexter Horton	1825 - 1904
184	Andrew Piper	1828 - 1904
197	James Osborne	1834 - 1881
199	Mrs. S. P. Smith	1808 - 1873
211	Catherine Maynard	1816 - 1906
211	David Swinson Maynard	1808 - 1873
216	Milton F. Densmore	1839 - 1908
218	William Meydenbauer	1832 - 1906
231	Samuel F. Coombs	1830 - 1908
233	Louis Wycoff	1830 - 1882
251	James Madison Colman	? - 1886
276	Jeffereson Davis Howell	1841 - 1875
276	Bruce Lee	1940 - 1973
276	Brandon Lee	1965 - 1993
292	Thomas Mercer	1813 - 1898
322	Charles C. Terry	1830 - 1866
328	John Pike	? - ?
342	Carson Boren	1824 - 1912
342	Arthur A. Denny	1822 - 1899
342	John Denny	1793 - 1875
342	Mary Boren Denny	1822 - 1910
342	Orion Denny	1853 - 1916

342	Rolland Denny	1851 - 1935
342	Sarah Latimer Boren Denny	1805 - 1888
360	Charles Plummer	1822 - 1866
364	Lyman Walter Bonney	1843 - 1922
364	Harry Watson	? - ?
379	John Webster	1816 - 1891
380	Edmund S. Meany	1862 - 1935
380	Josiah Settle	1814 - 1876
401	Abigail Holgate Hanford	1824 - 1905
401	Cornelius Holgate Hanford	1849 - 1926
401	Edward Hanford	1807 - 1884
401	Milton Holgate	1841 - 1856
416	John H. McGilvra	1827 - 1903
417	Rev. George Whitworth	1816 - 1907
420	Ossian Carr	1832 - 1912
420	E.S. Ingraham	1805 - 1905
422	Sophie Frye Bass	1866 - 1947
422	George F. Frye	1833 - 1912
422	Louisa Catherine Denny Frye	1844 - 1924
422	Roberta Frye Watt	1875 - 1963
432	Henry Van Asselt	1817 - 1902
437	James Lowman	1856 - 1947
459	James Colman	1832 - 1906
470	Nils Jacob Olhm	1828 - 1898
496	Granville Haller	1819 - 1897
506	Eliza Mercer Graham	1840 - 1862
506	Katherine Stickney Graham	1805 - 1901
540	Austin Americus Bell	1854 - 1889
550	Nora Johns Hill	1837 - 1855
552	Mary Ann Boyer Conklin	1821 - 1873
552	William Castro	? - 1864
554	John Buckley	1798 - 1874
560	Carl Larson Maple	? - 1905
566	David Maurer	1811 - 1873
580	William Renton	1818 - 1905
926	Lou Graham	1857 - 1903
1147	Robert Moran	1857 - 1943

EE	Elisha P. Ferry	1825 - 1895
EE	John Leary	1837 - 1905
K	Henry A. Atkins	1827 - 1885
L	Gardner Kellogg	1839 - 1918
M	Oliver C. Shorey	1831 - 1900

INDEX

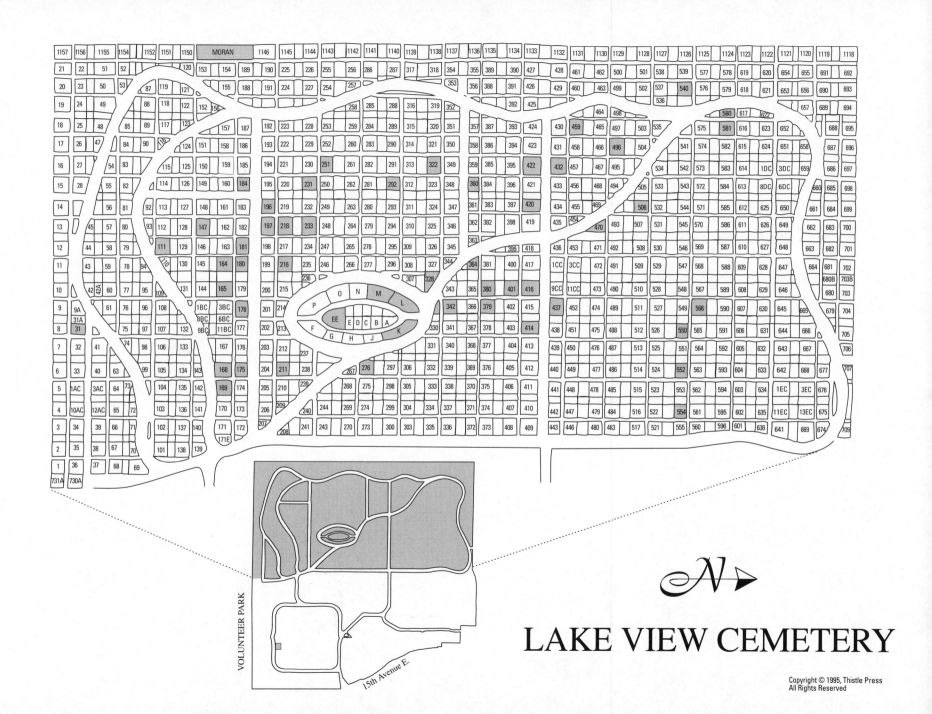

LAKE VIEW CEMETERY